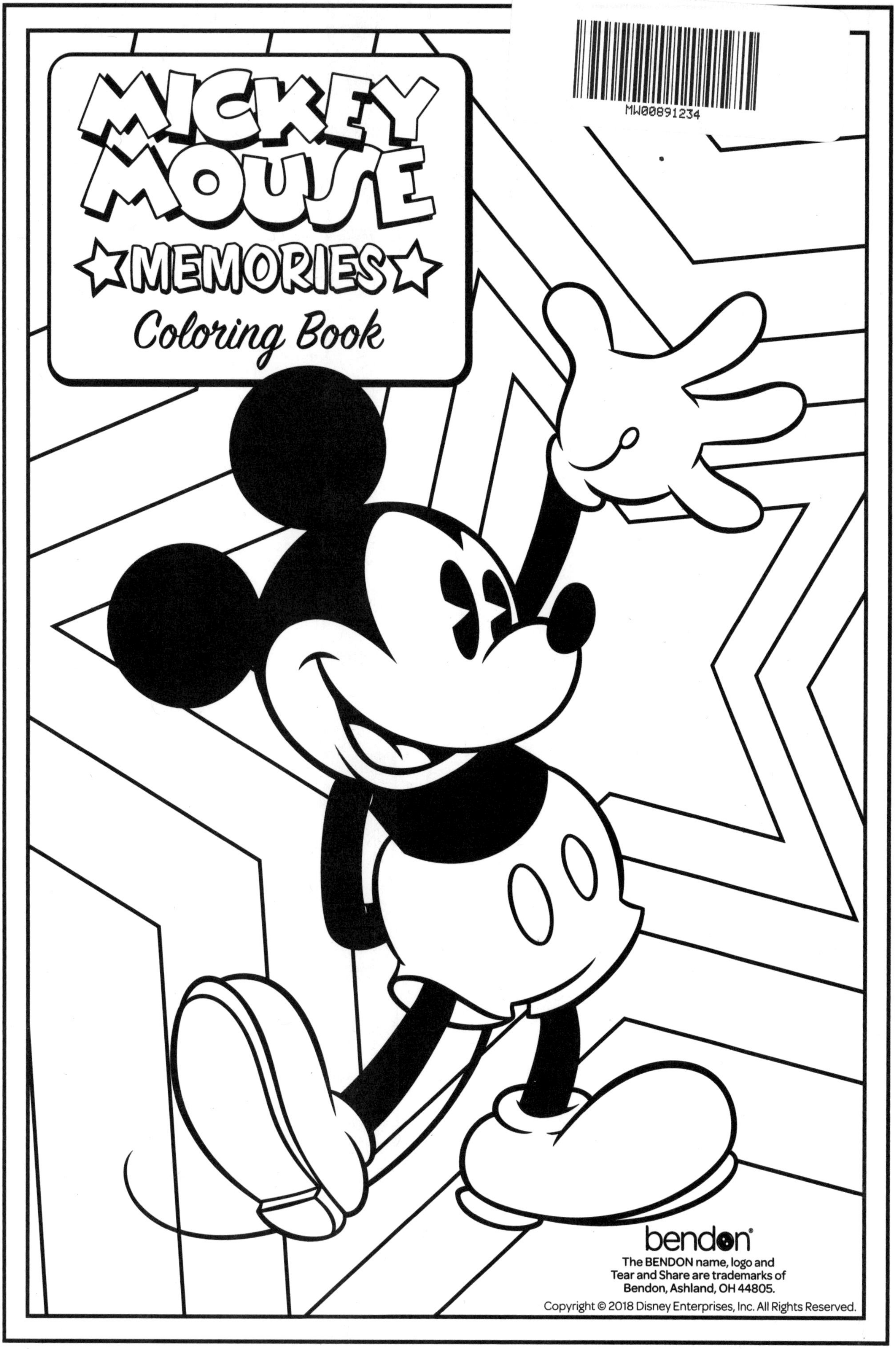

bendon
The BENDON name, logo and
Tear and Share are trademarks of
Bendon, Ashland, OH 44805.

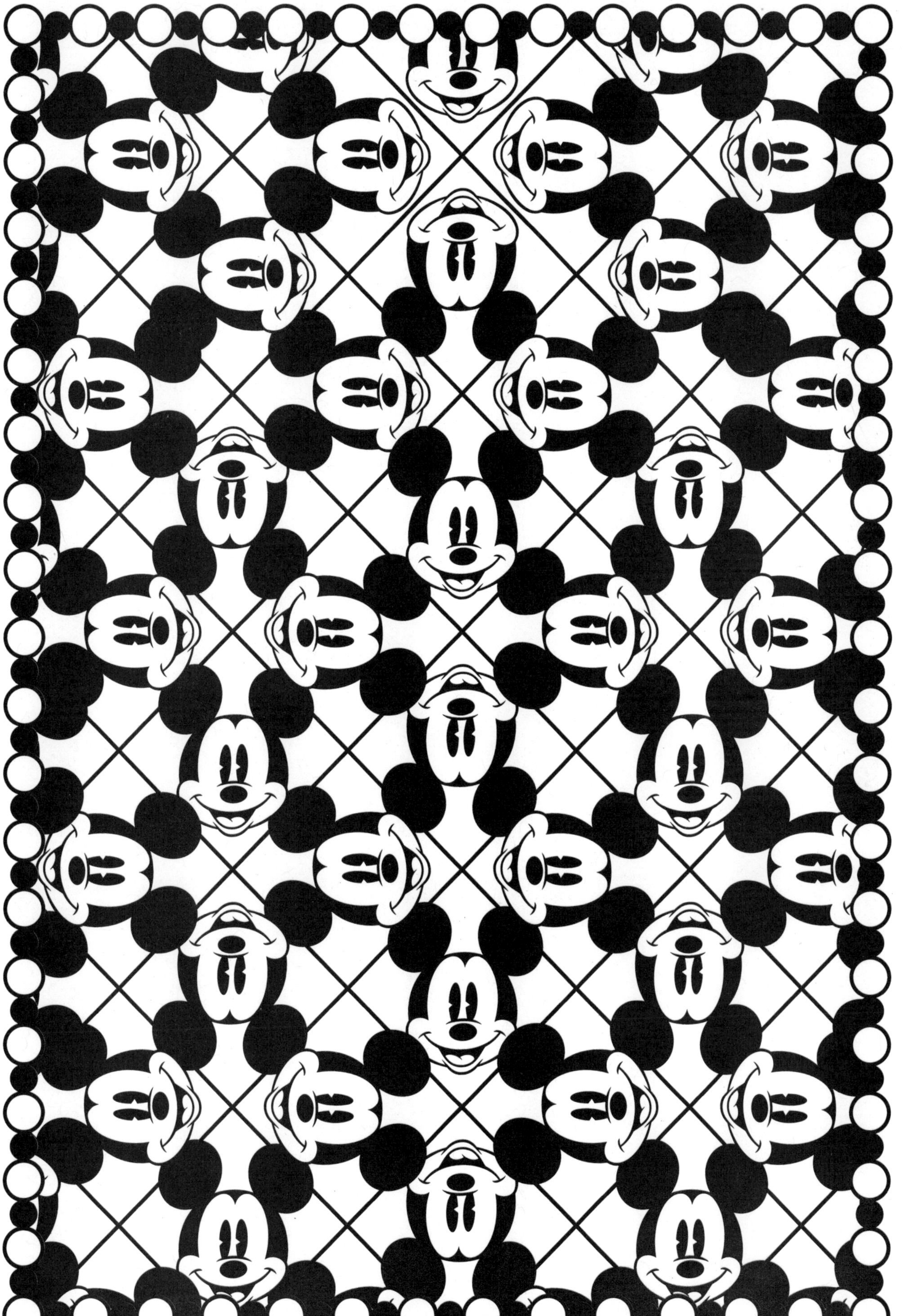

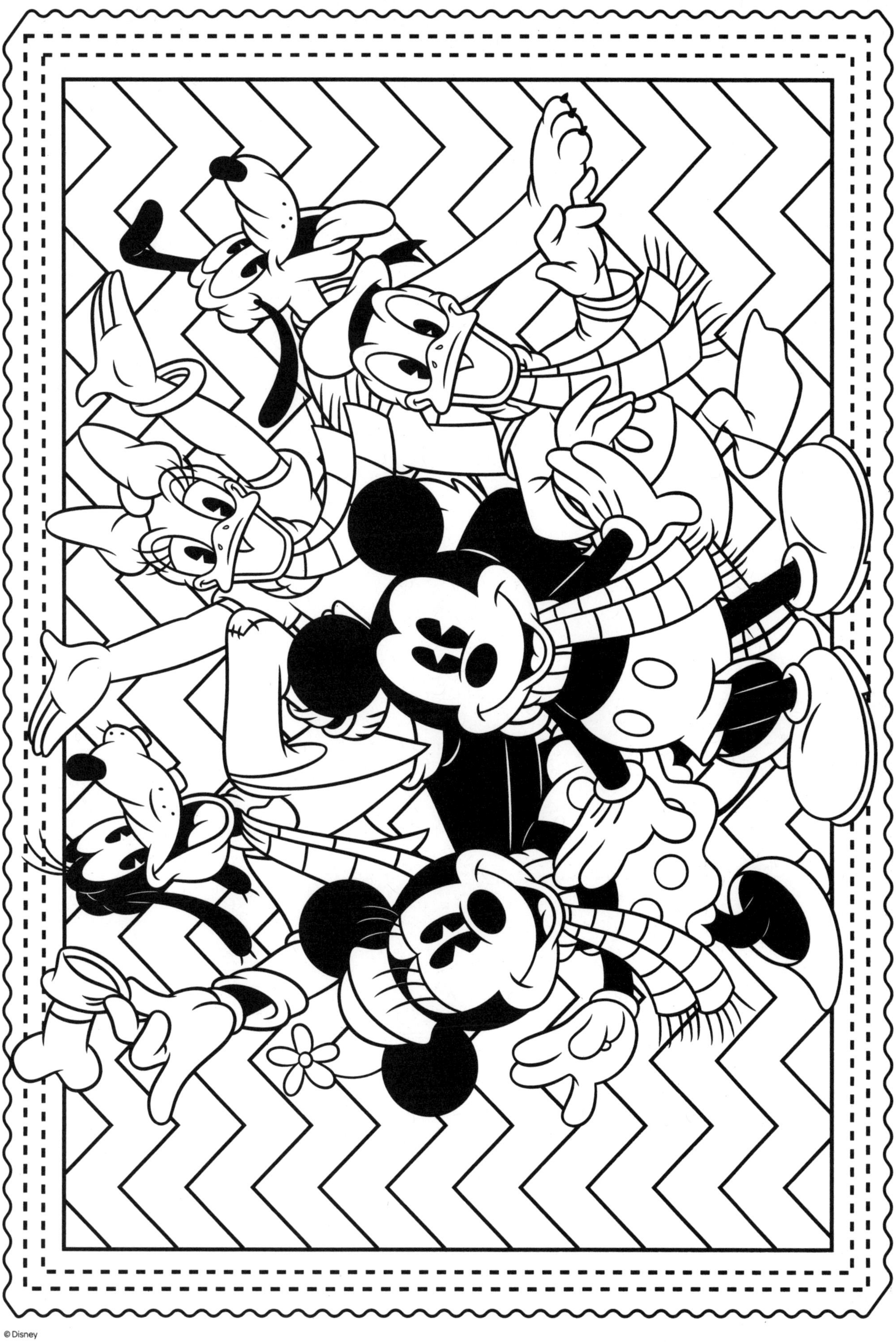

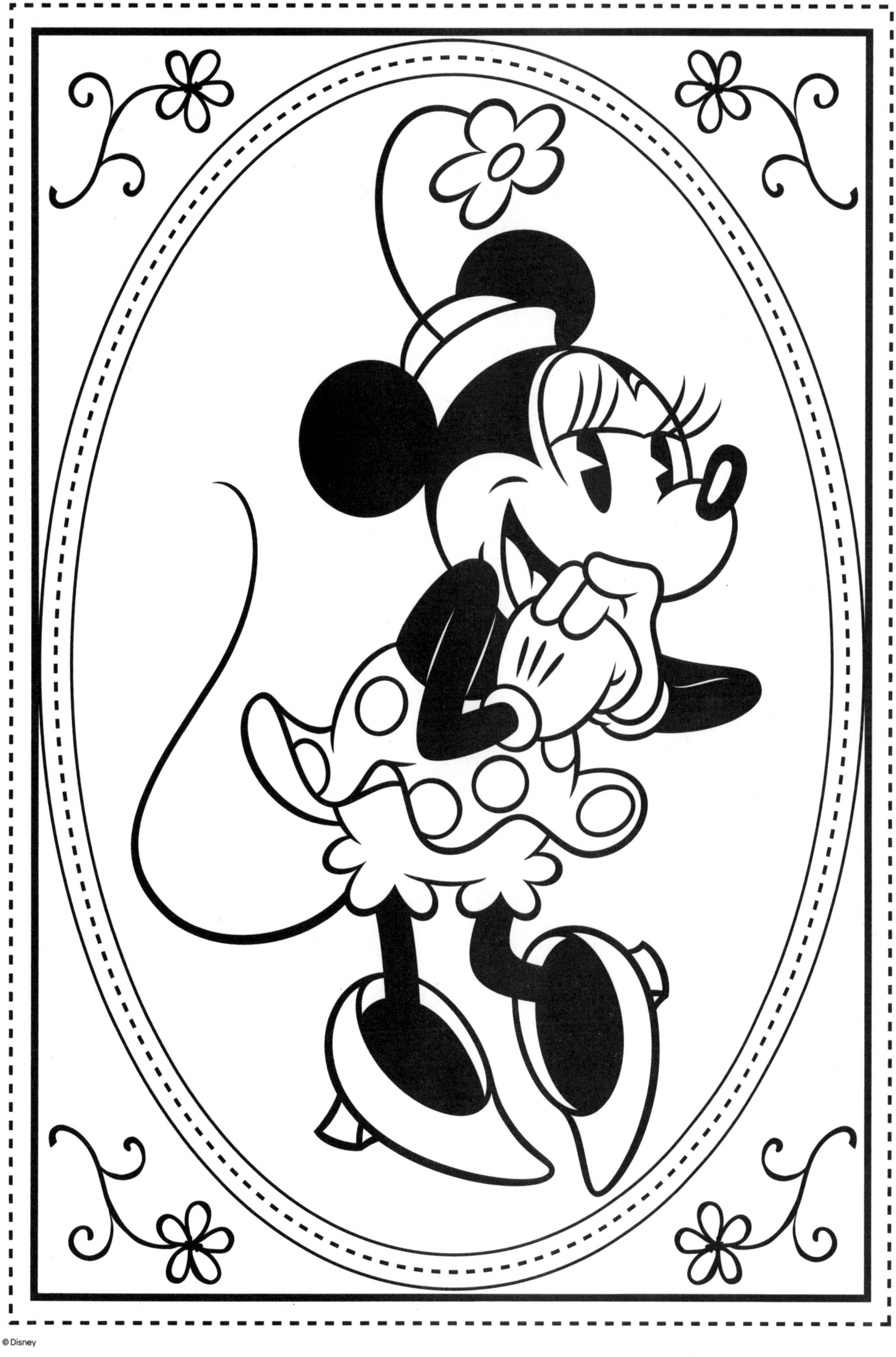

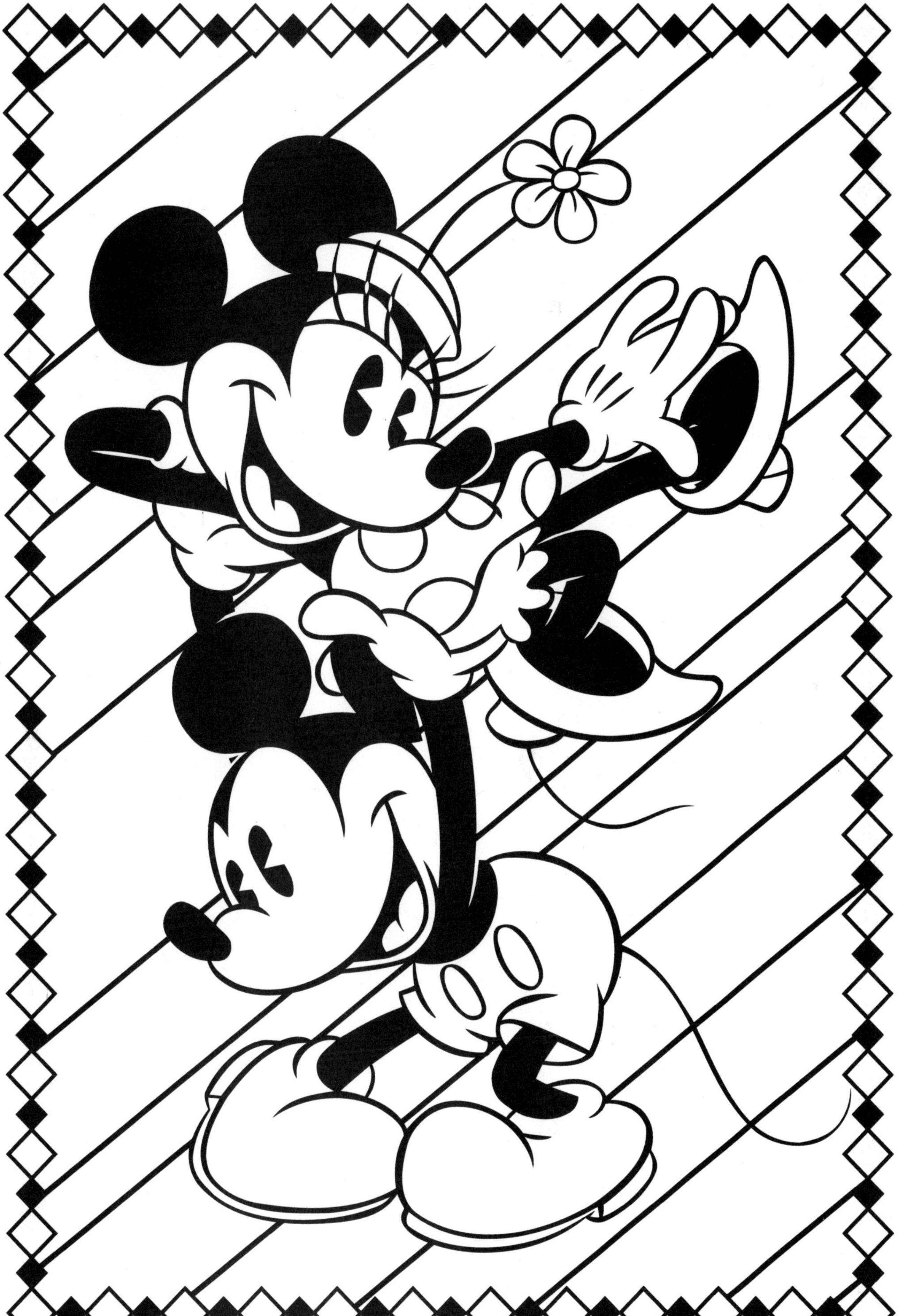

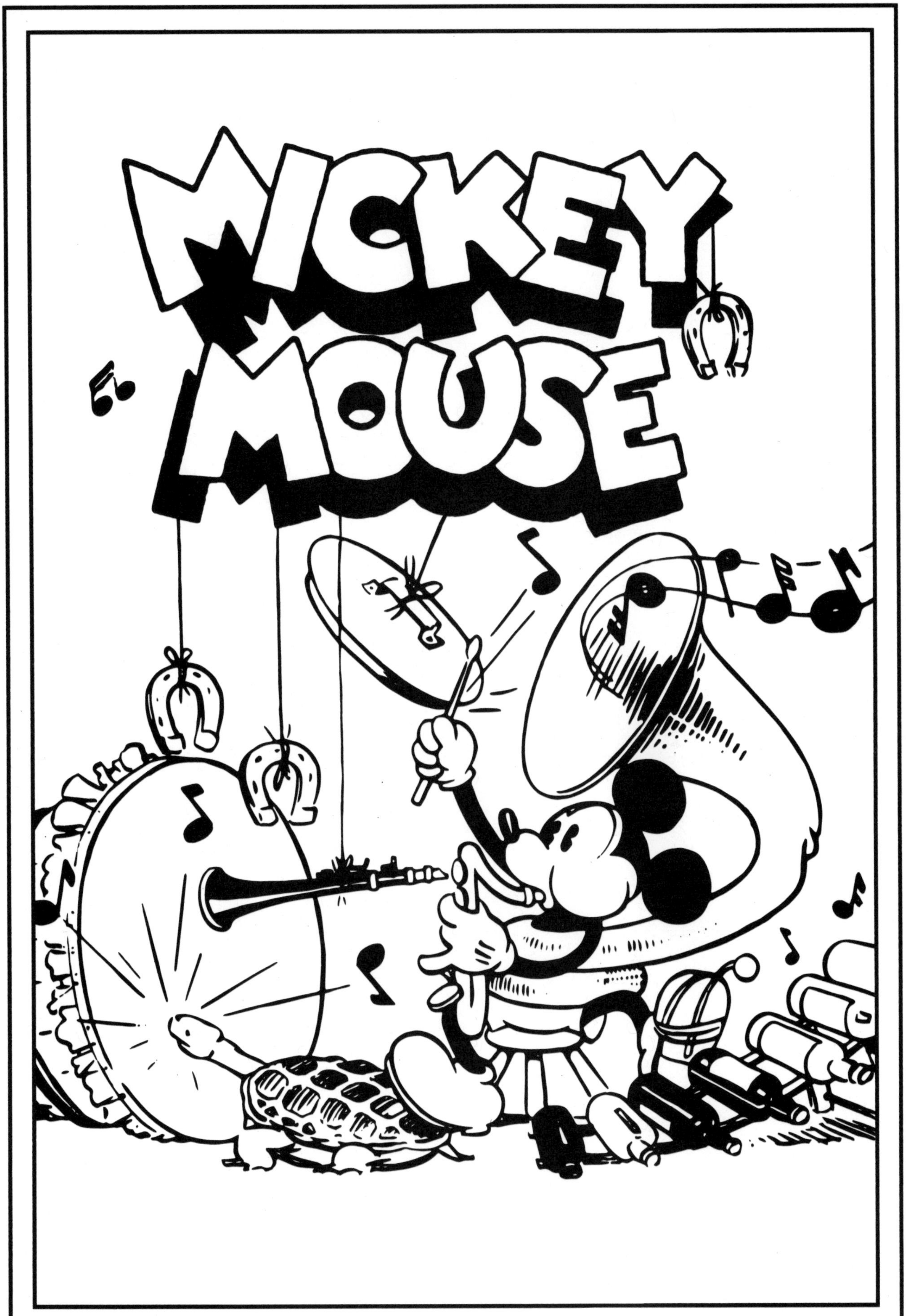
MICKEY
MOUSE

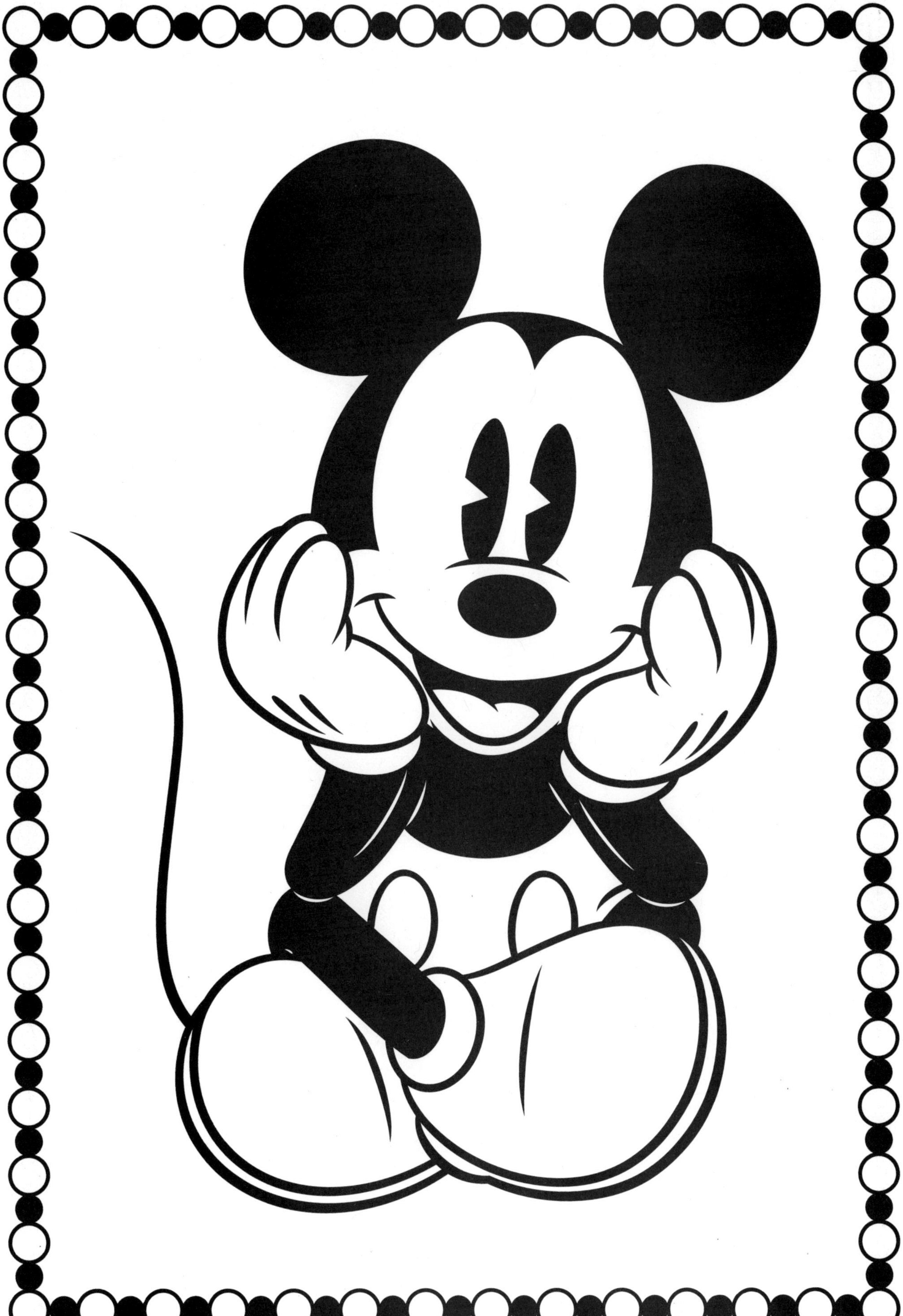

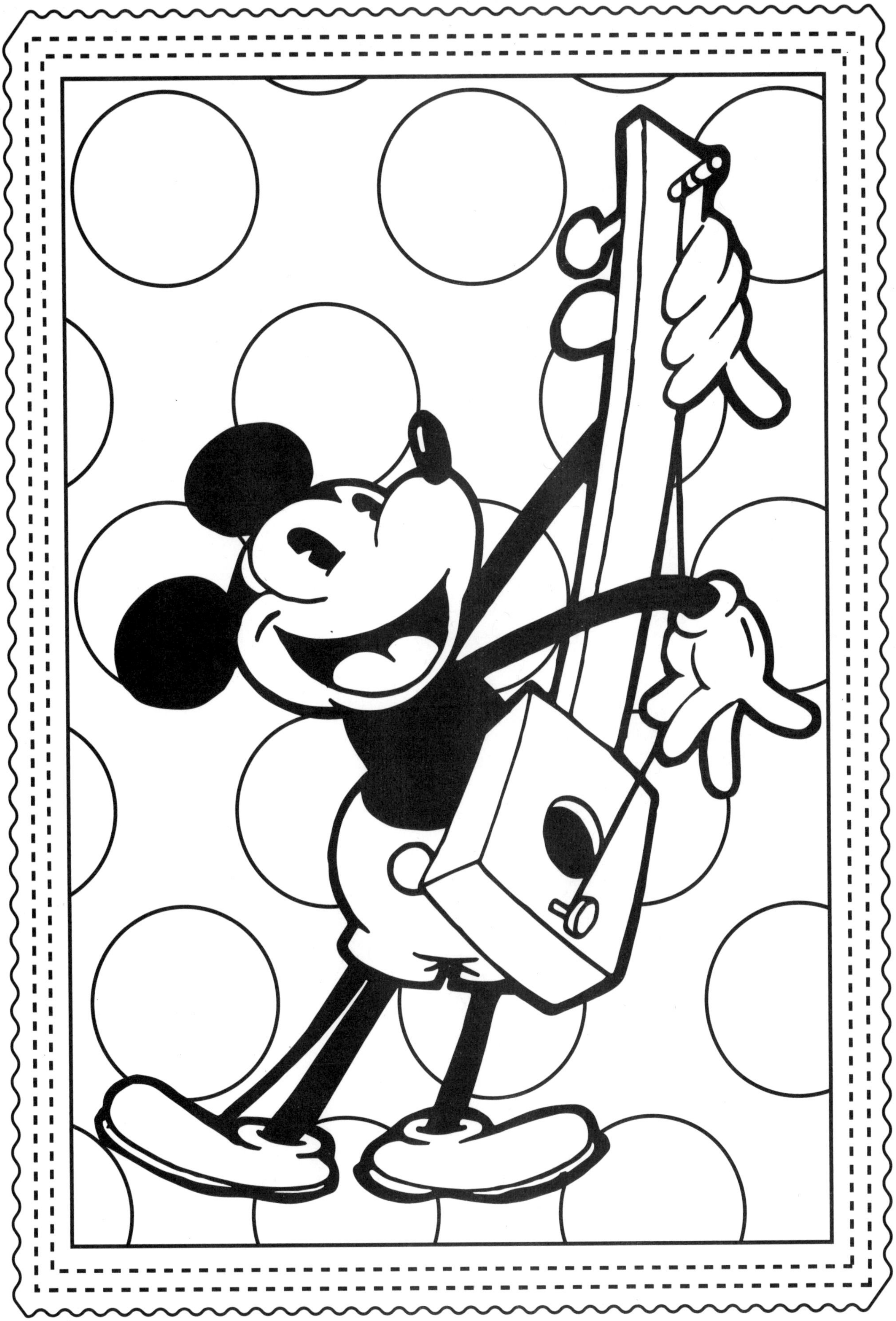

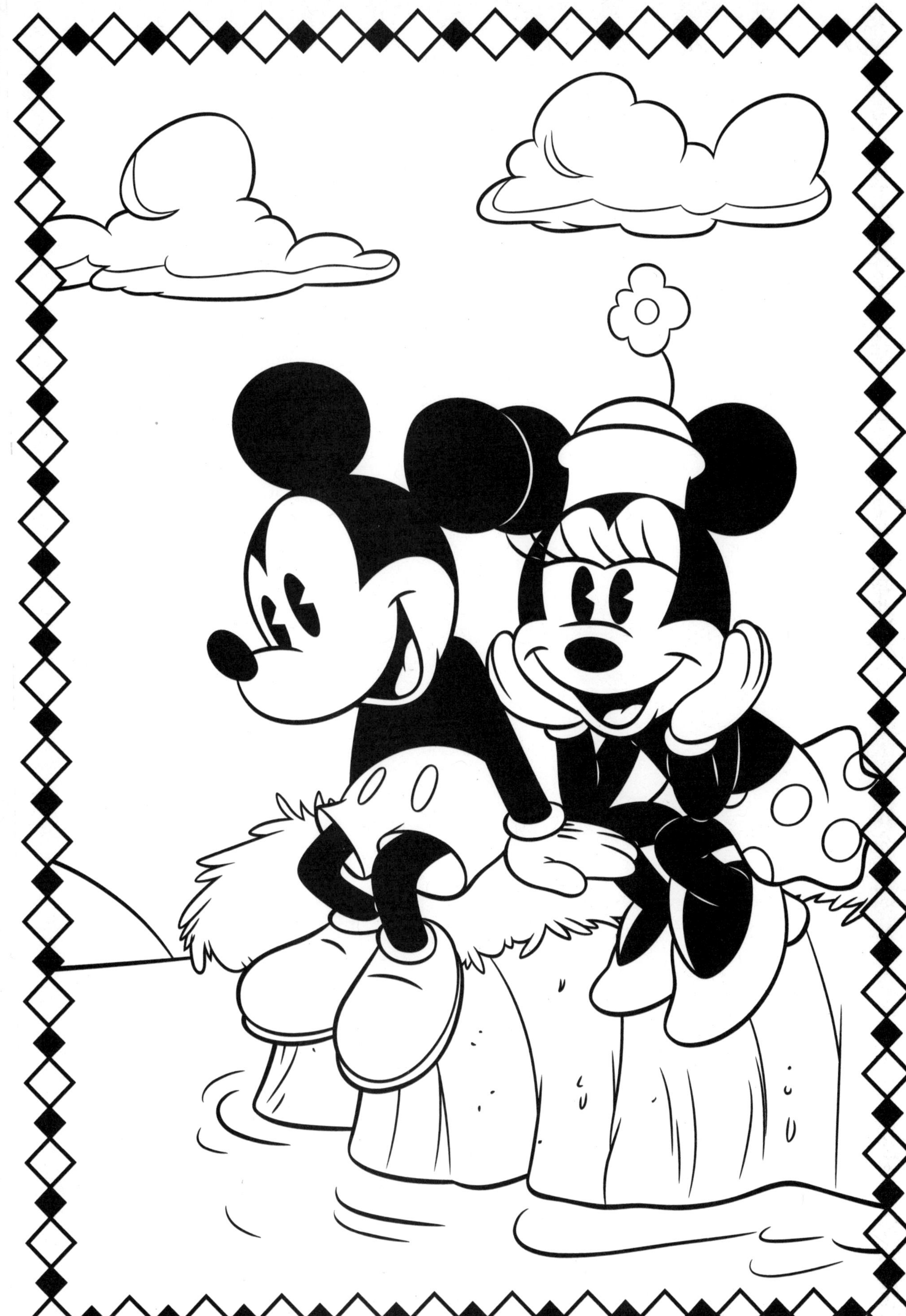

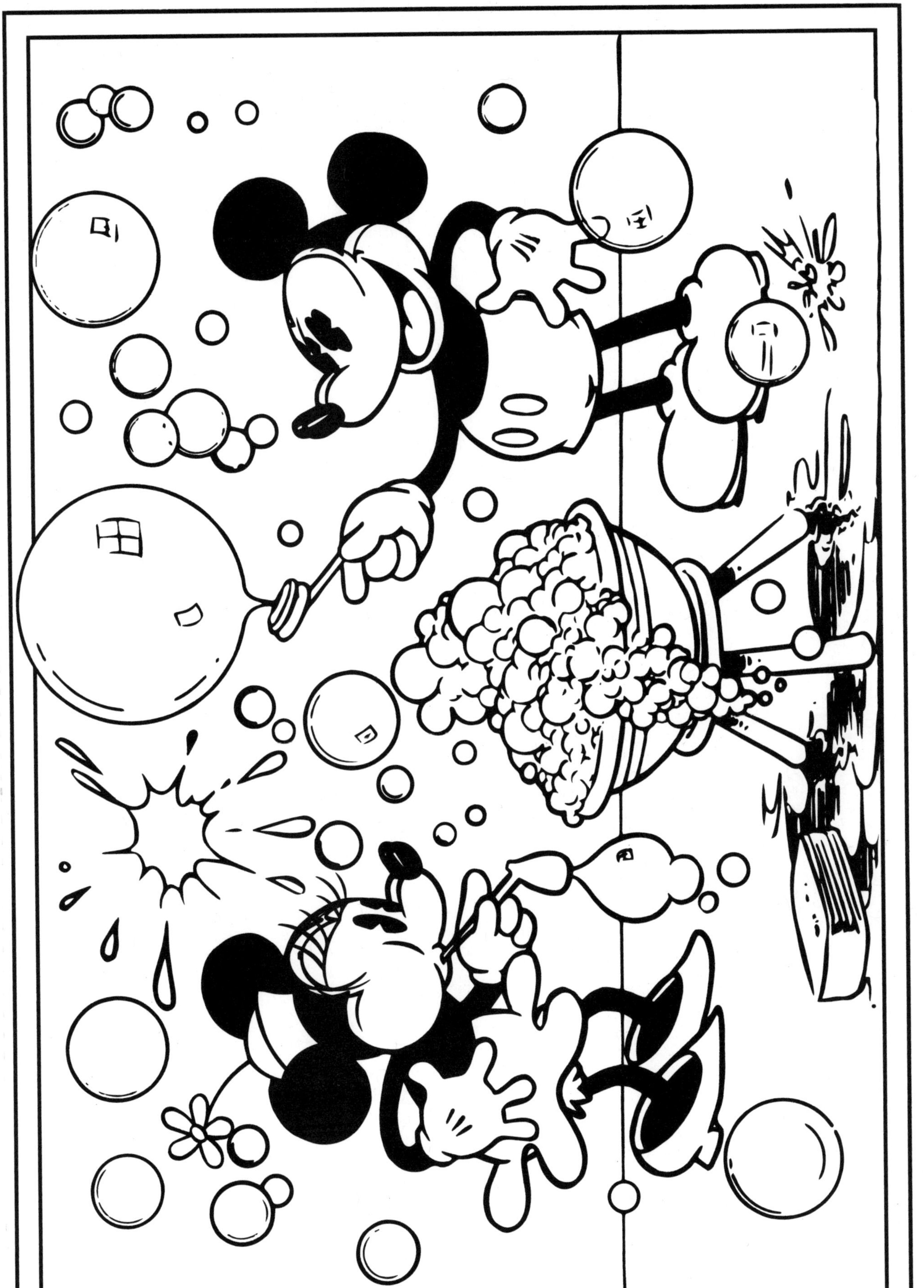

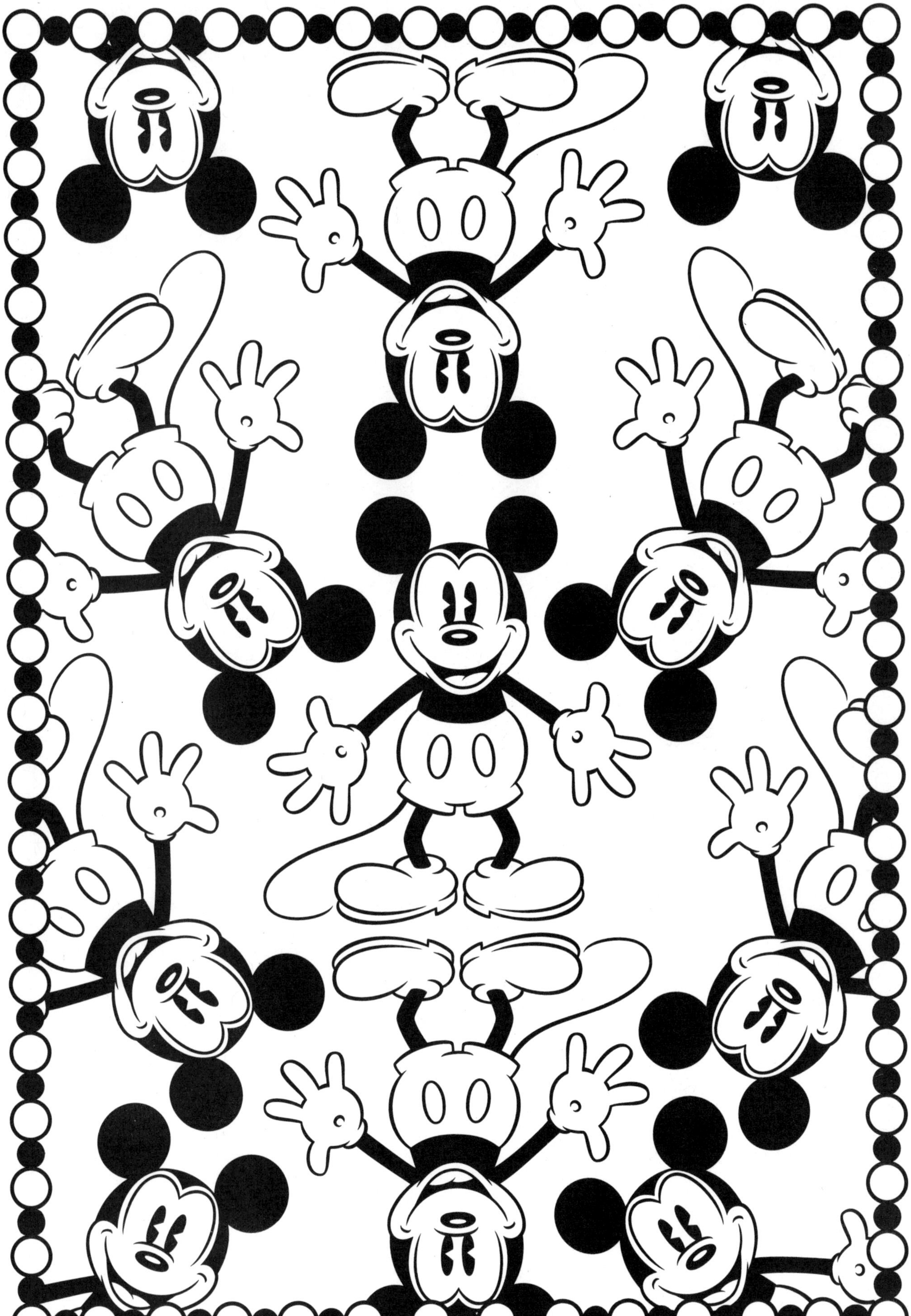

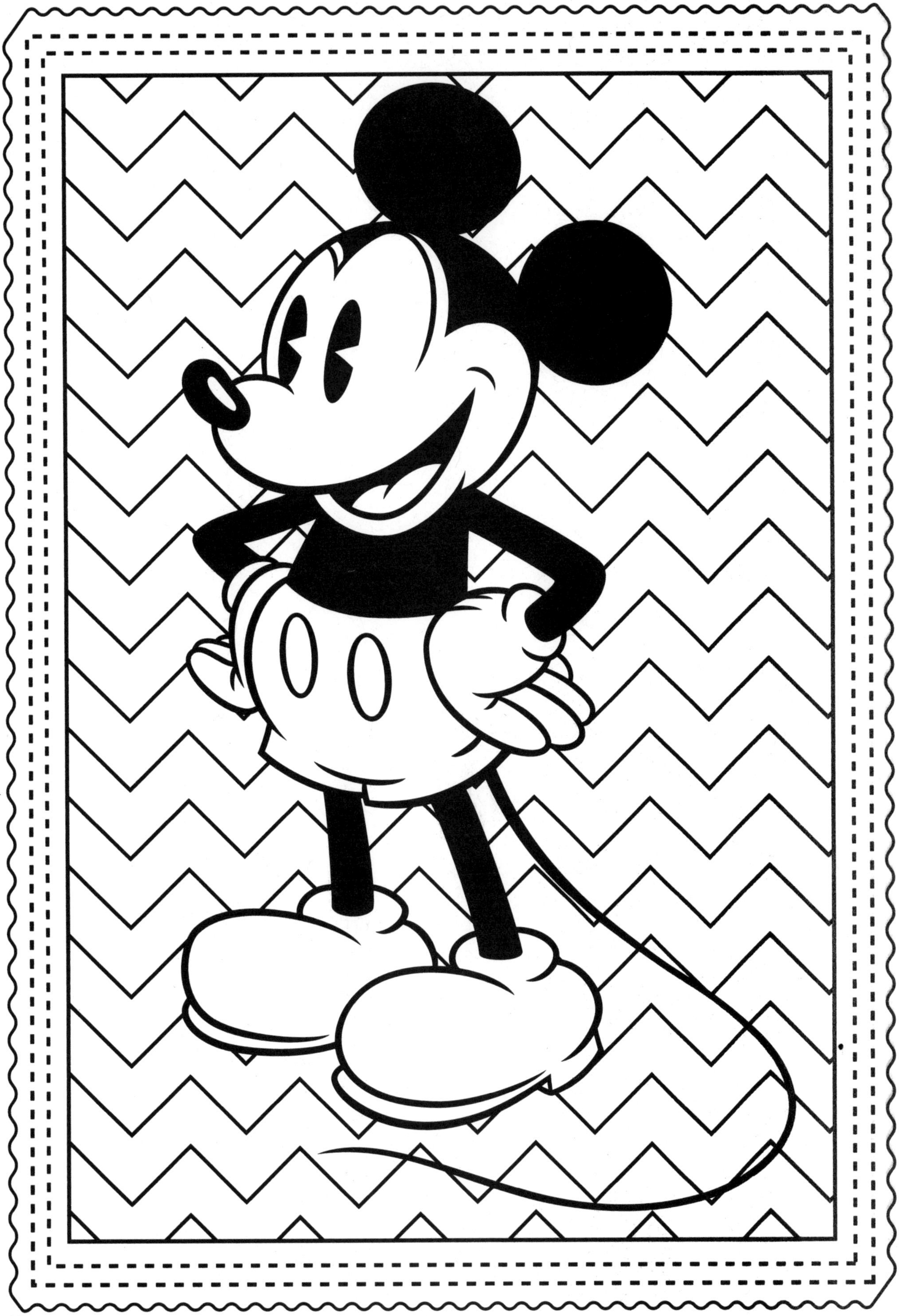

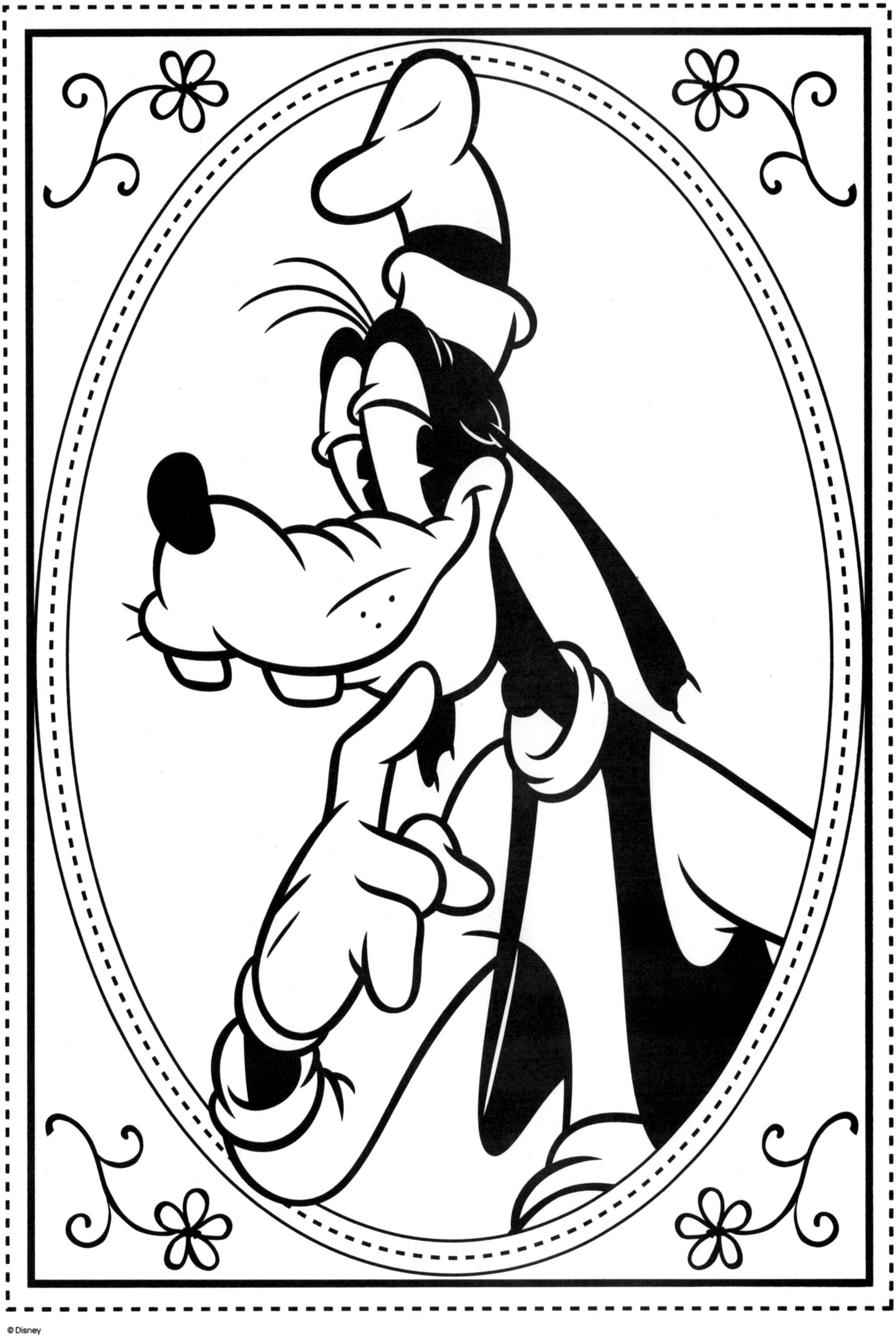

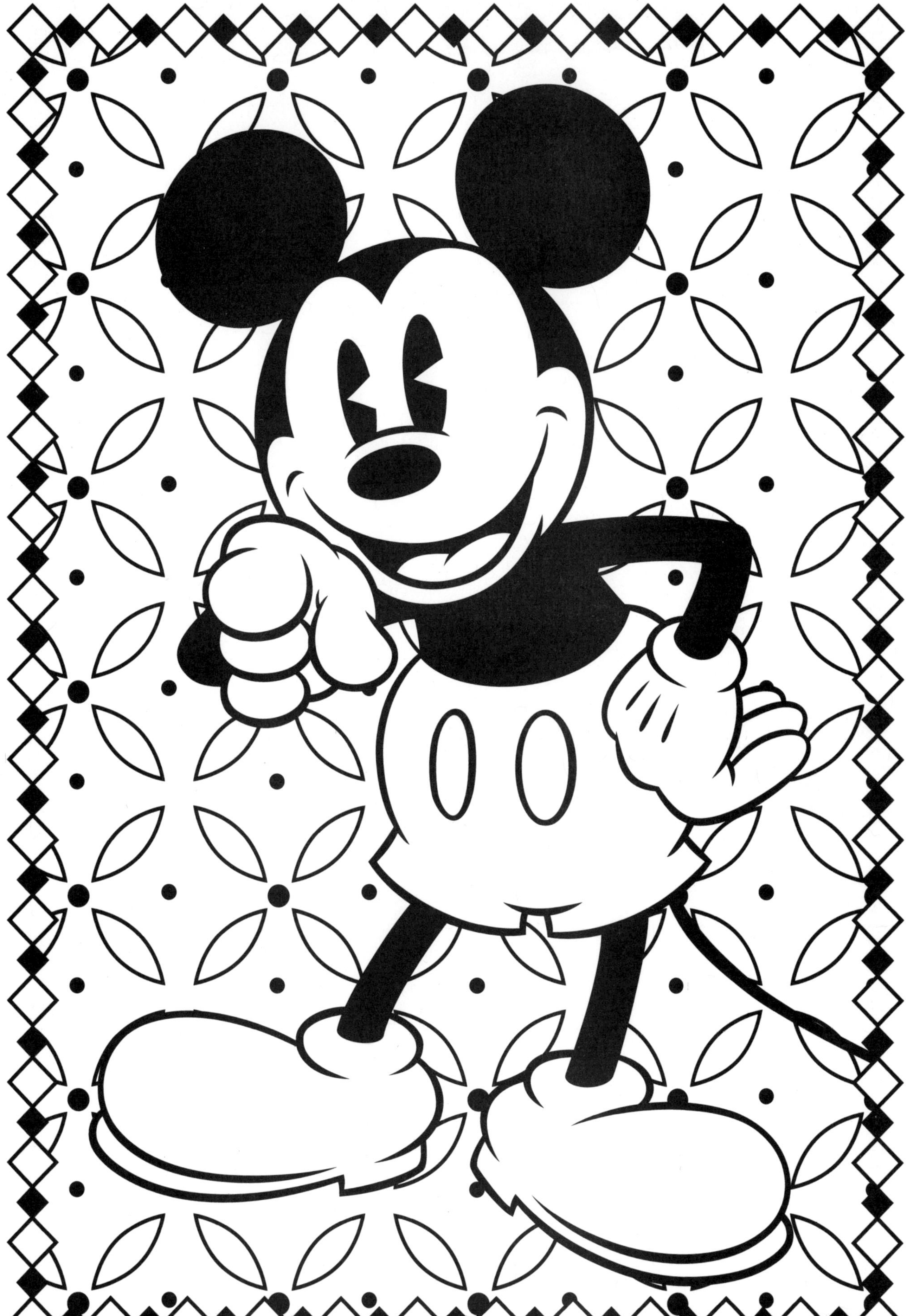

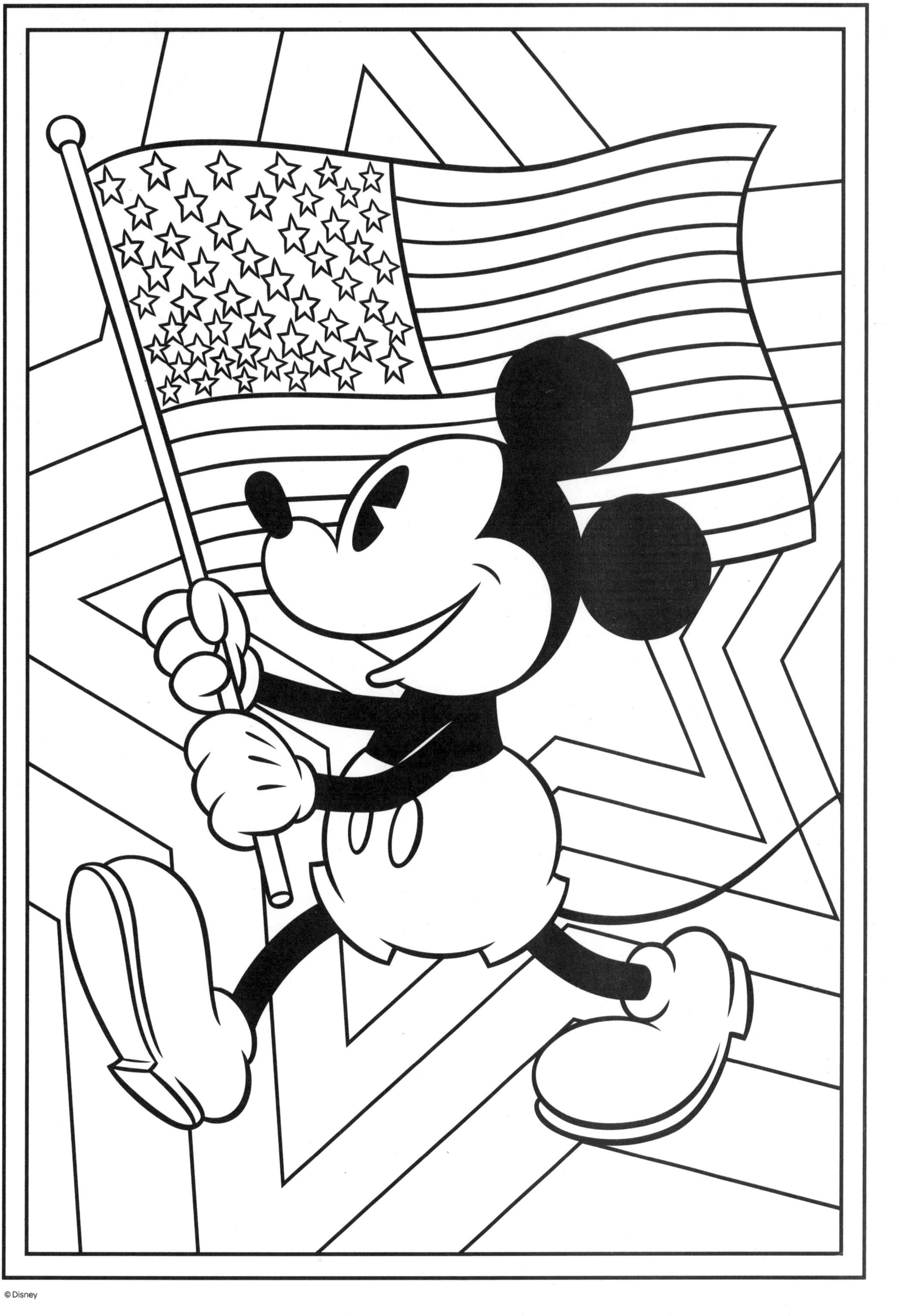

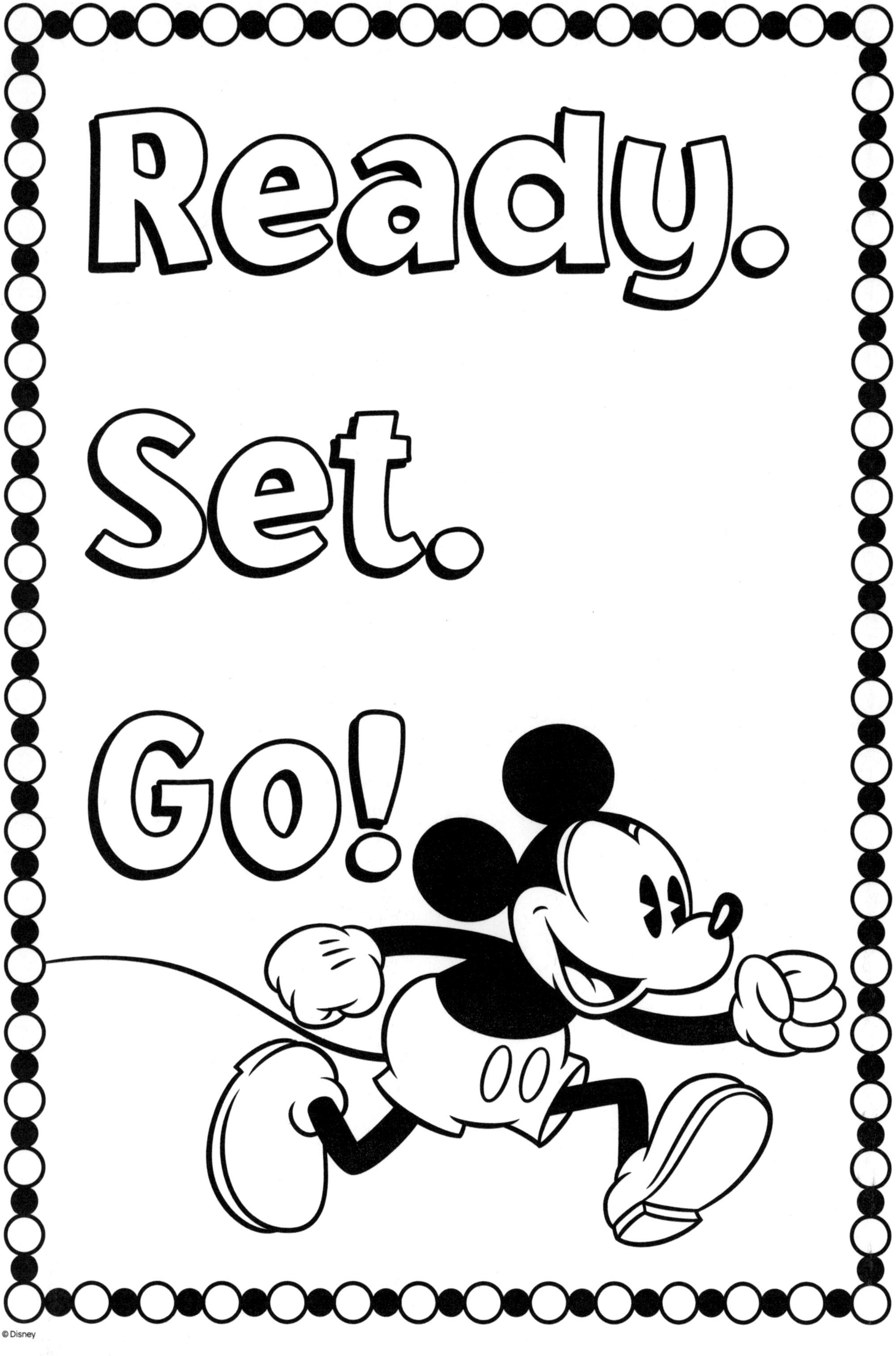
Ready.
Set.
Go!

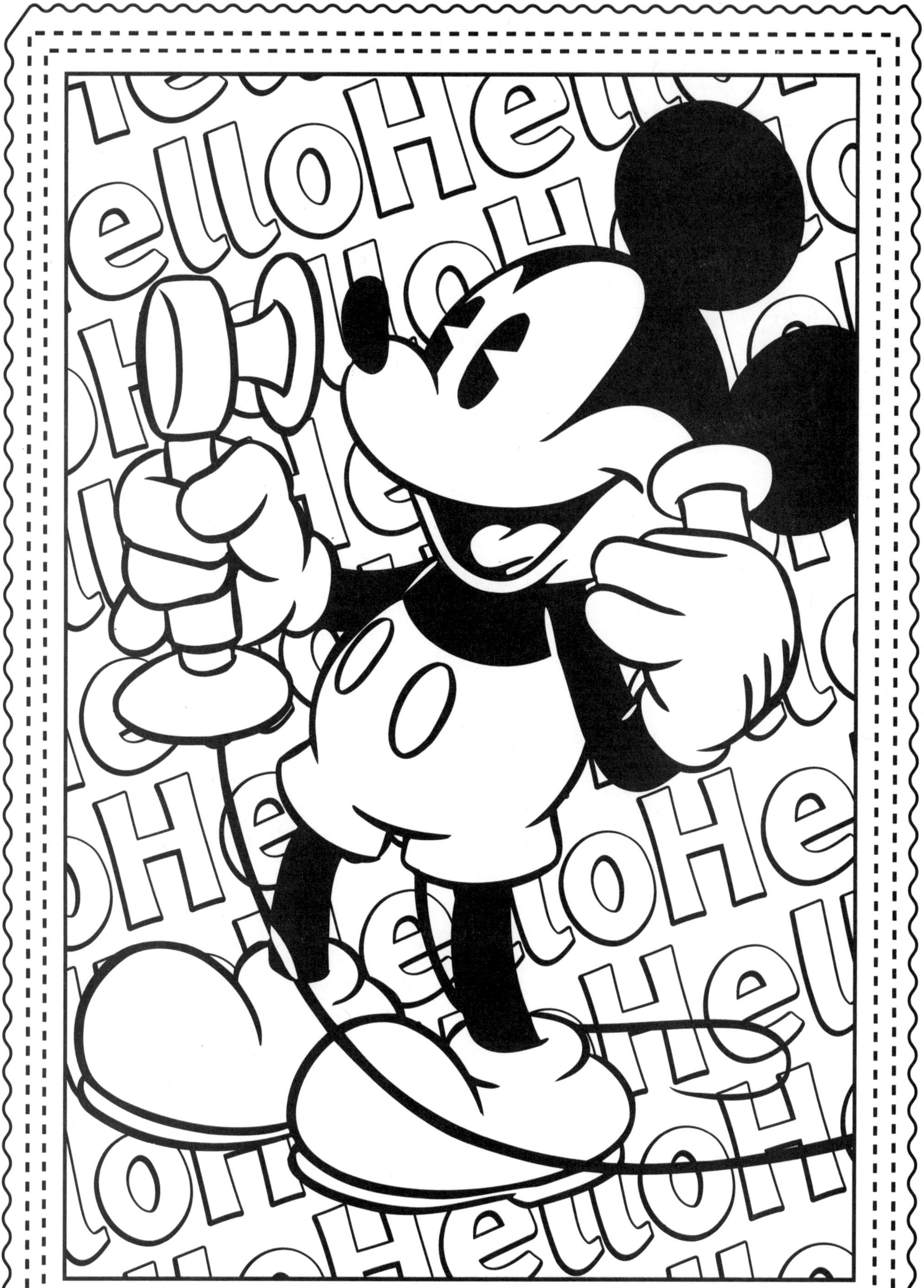

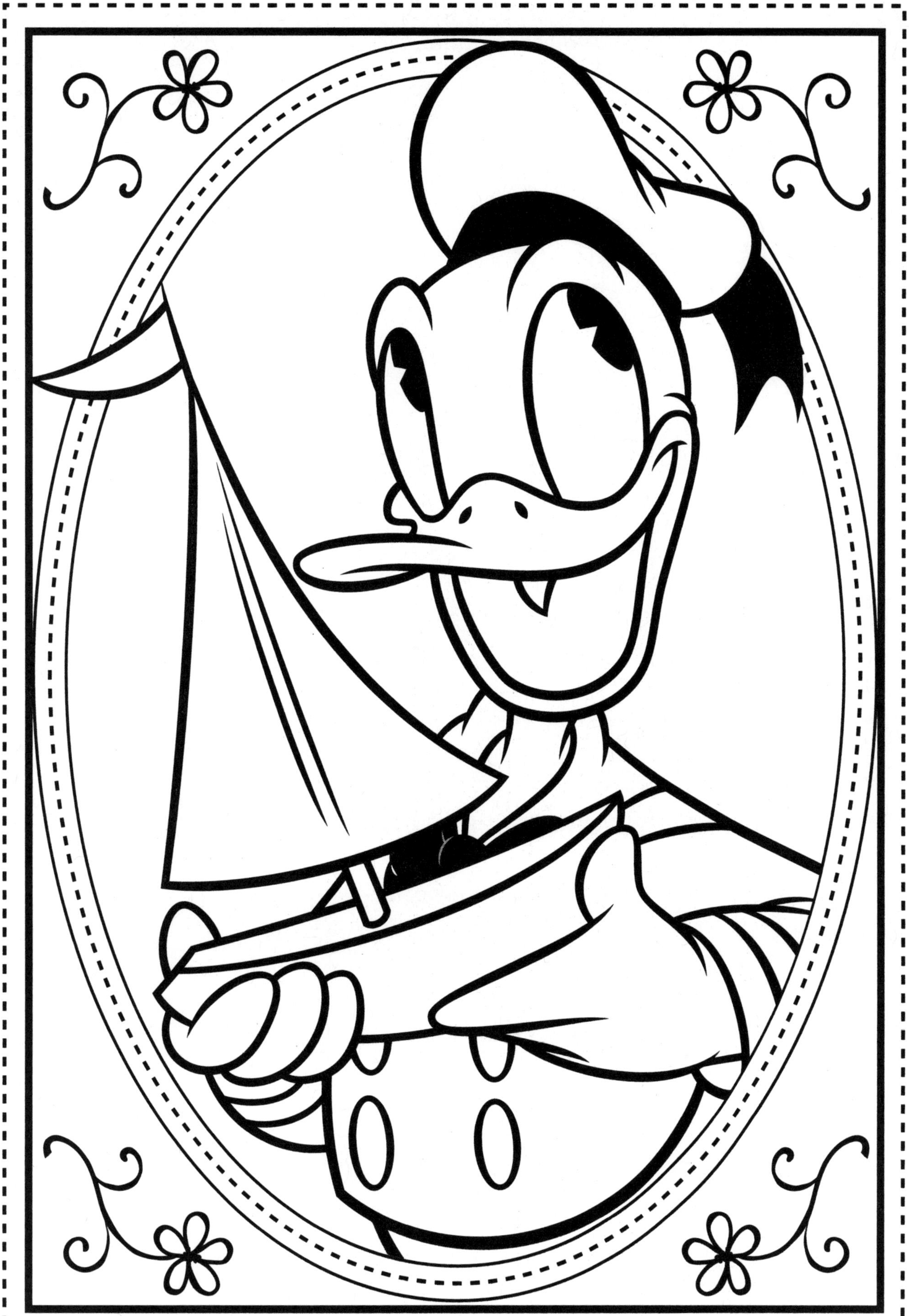

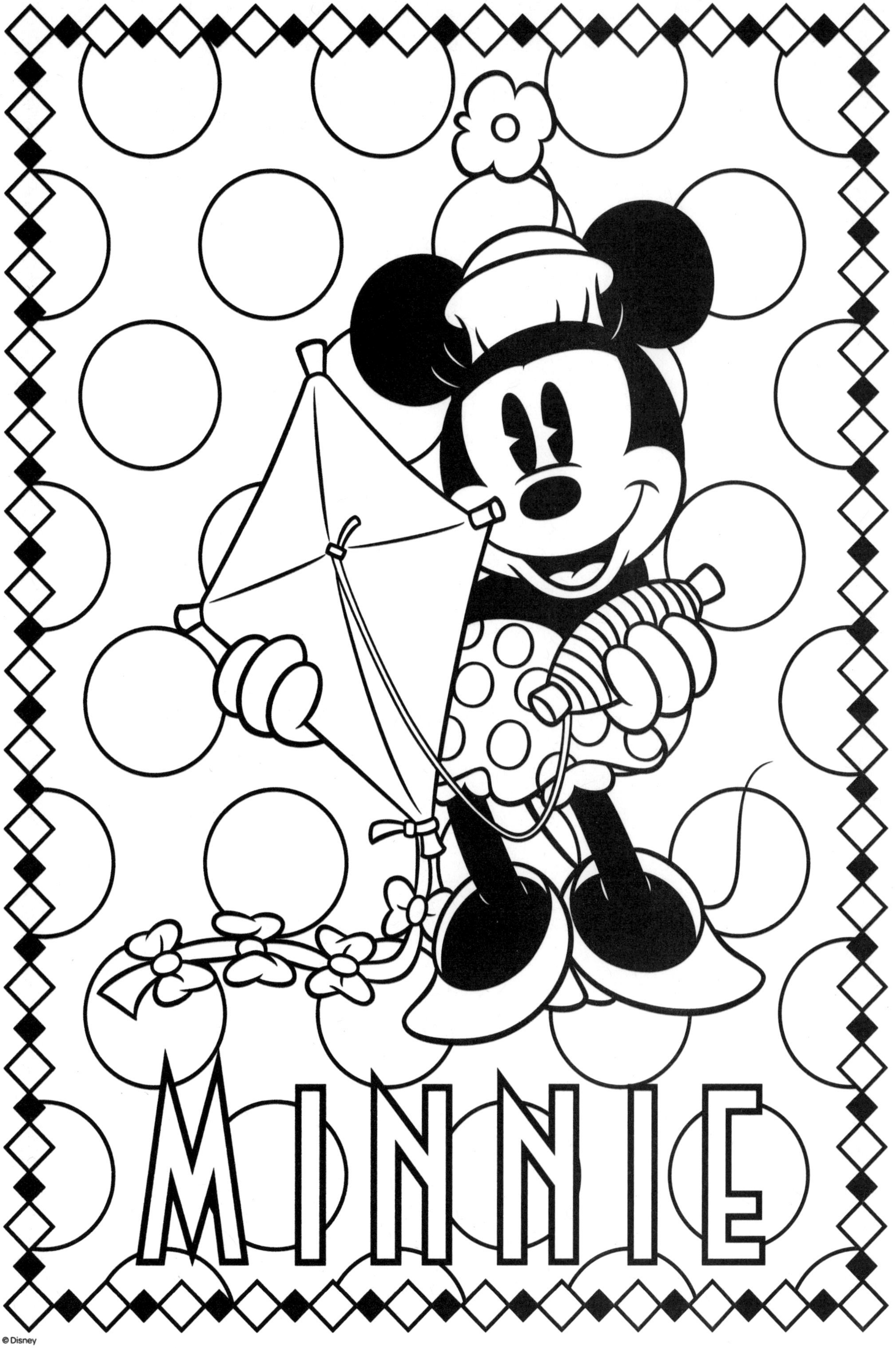
MINNIE

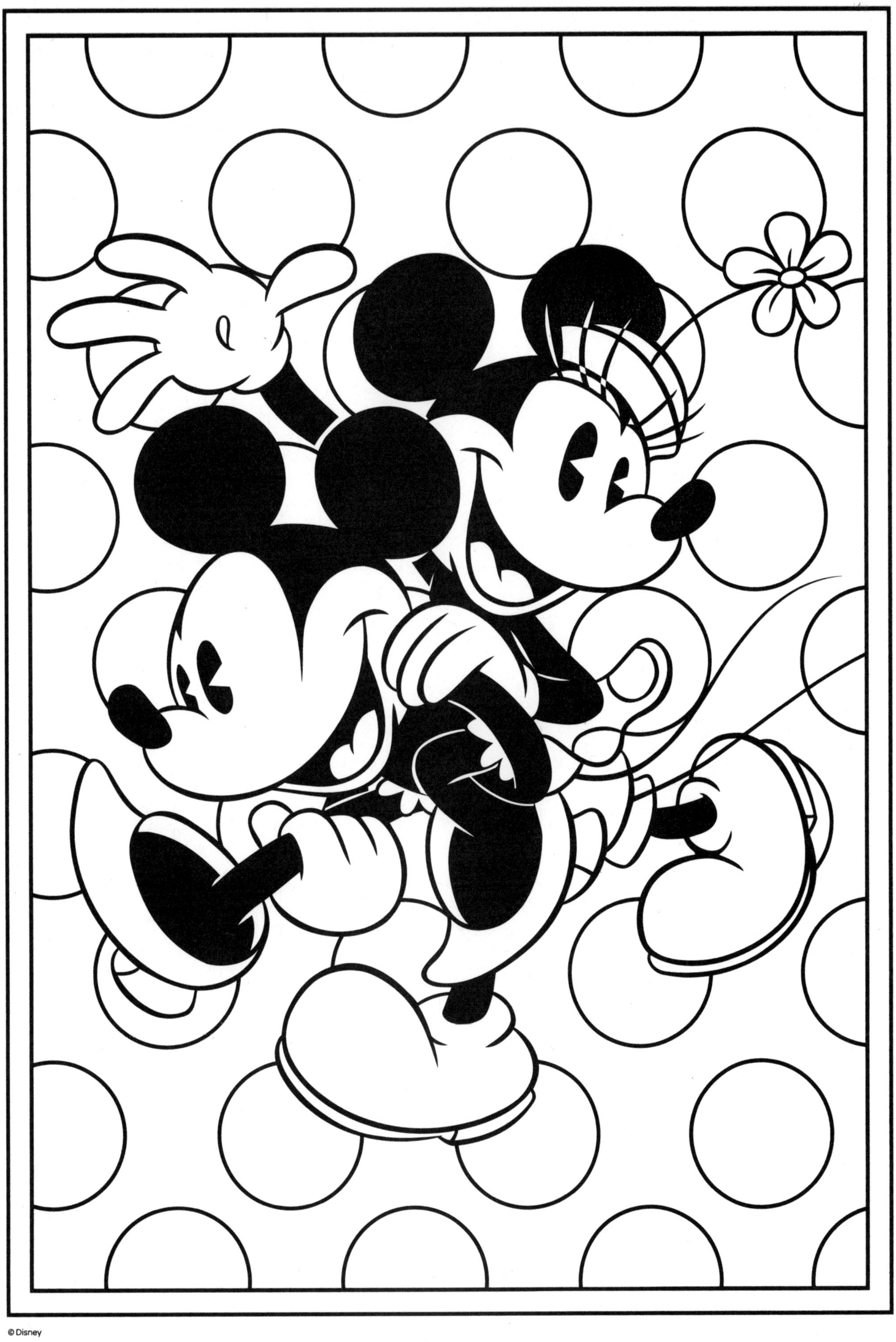

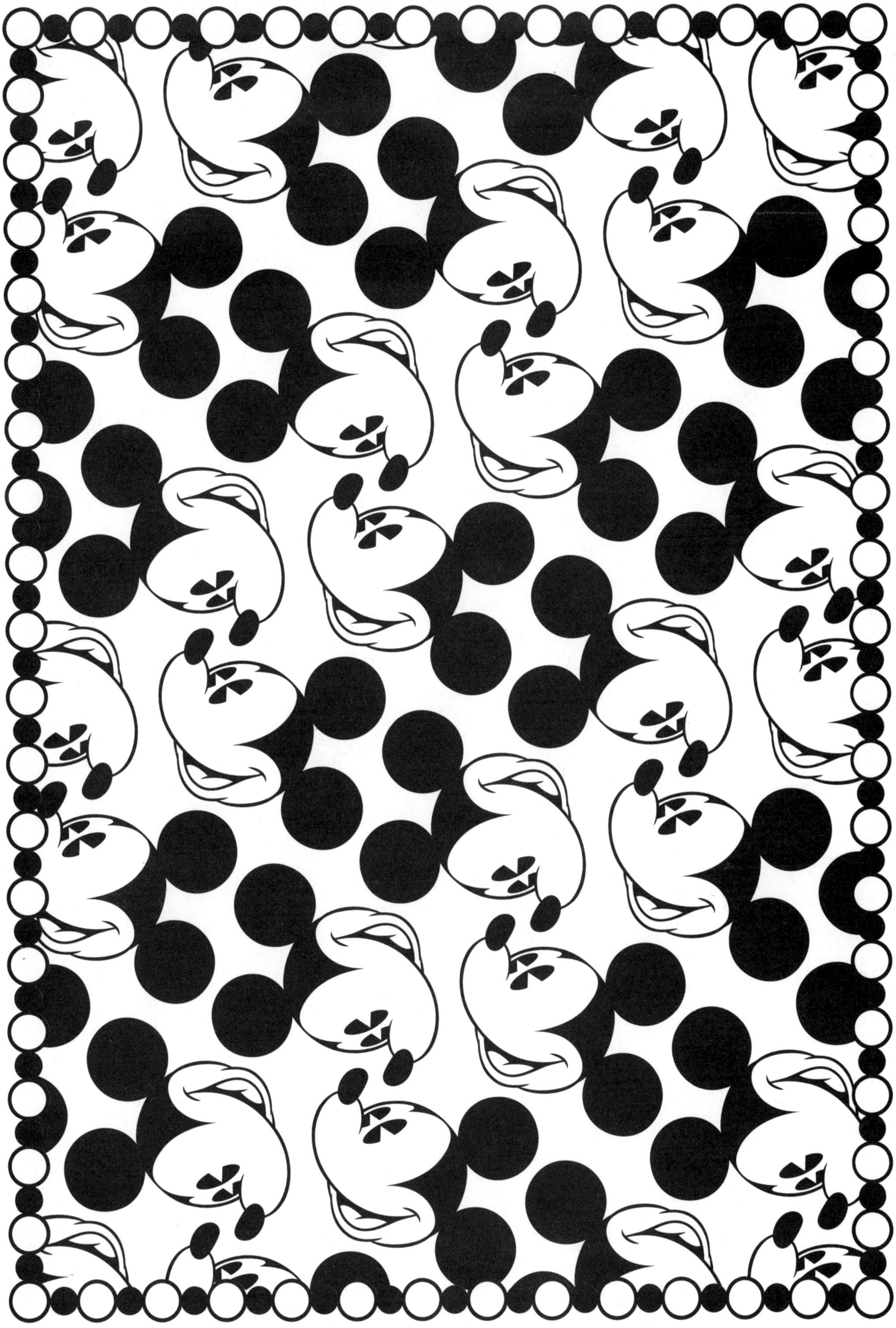

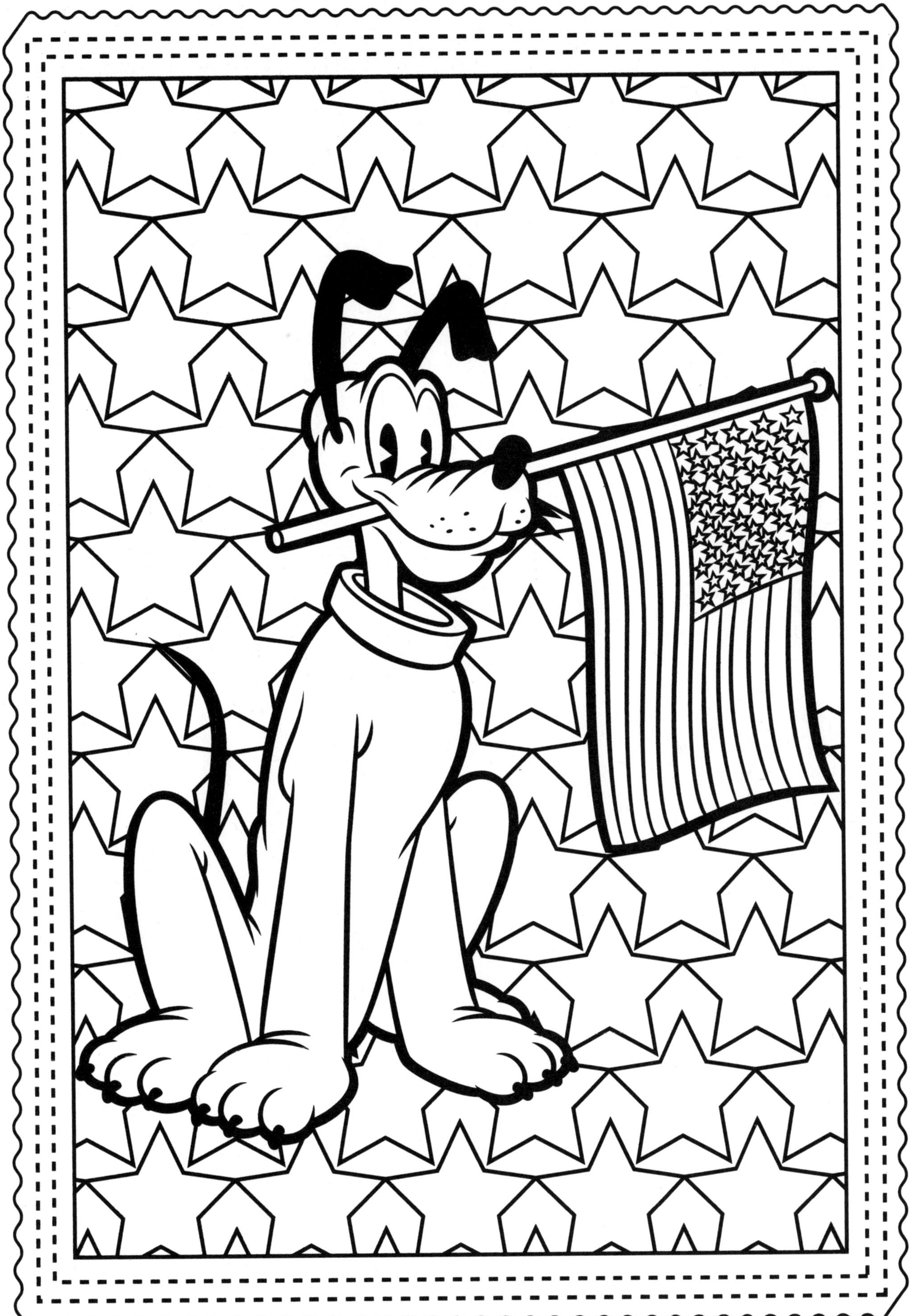

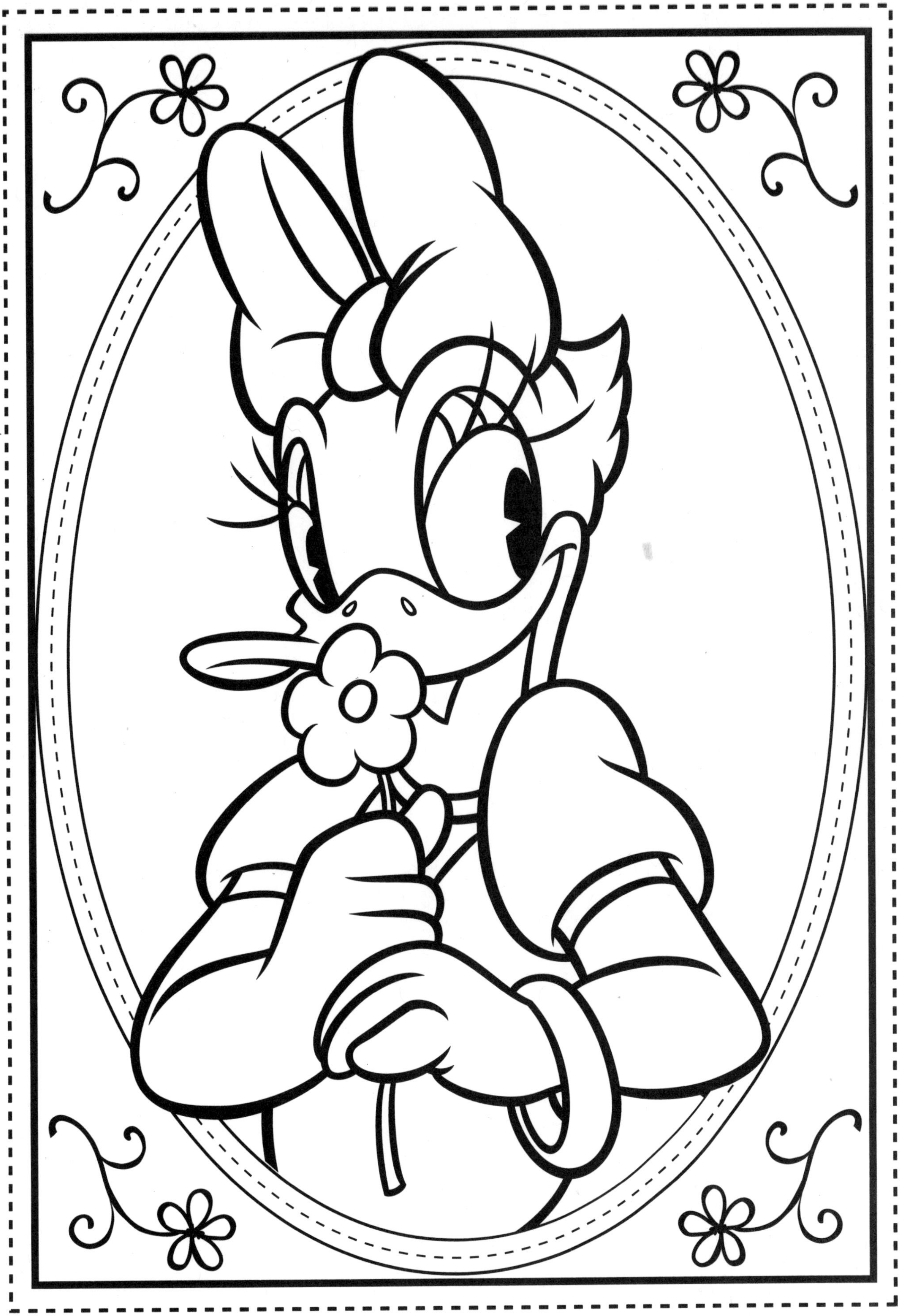

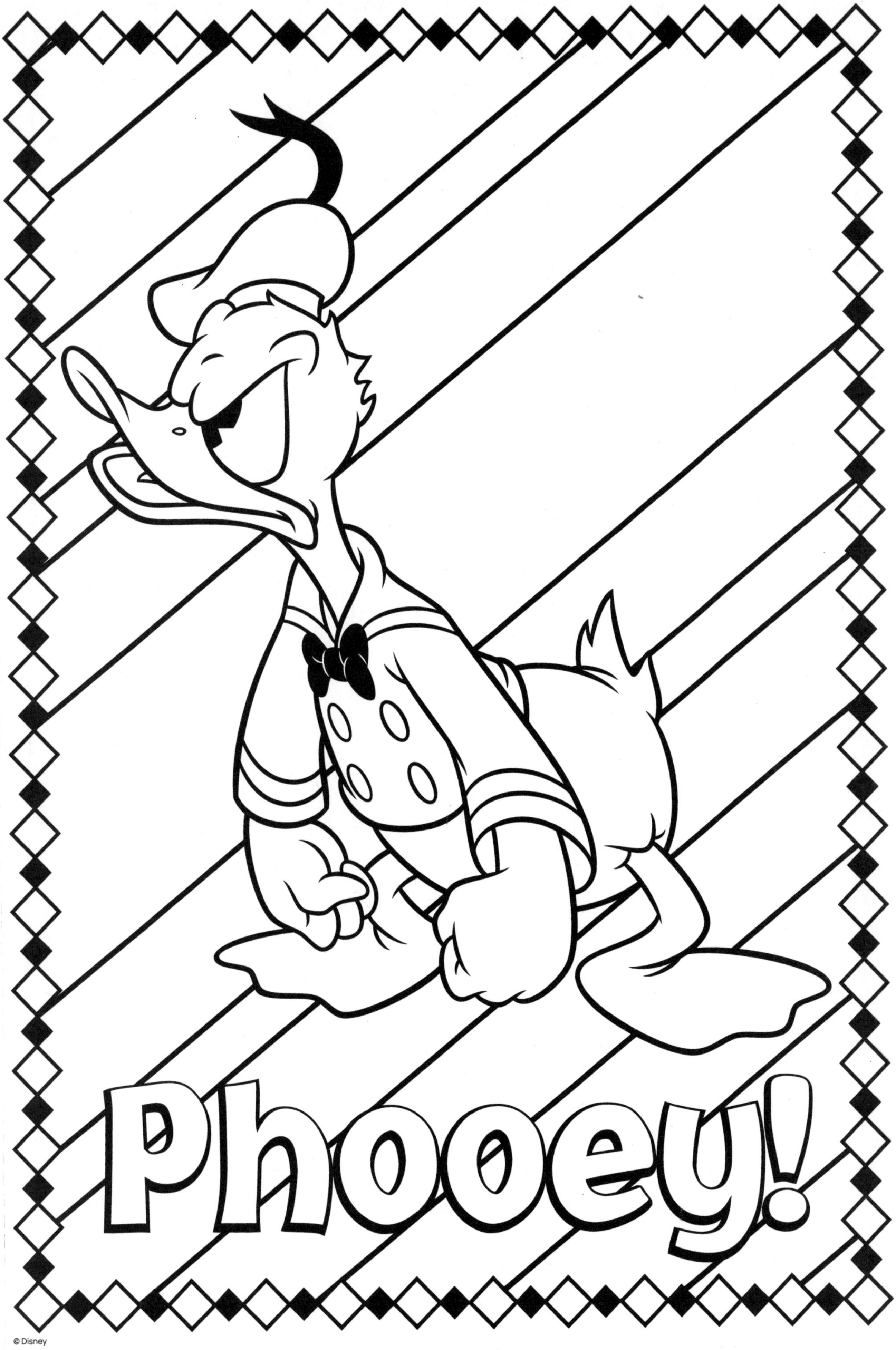
Phooey!

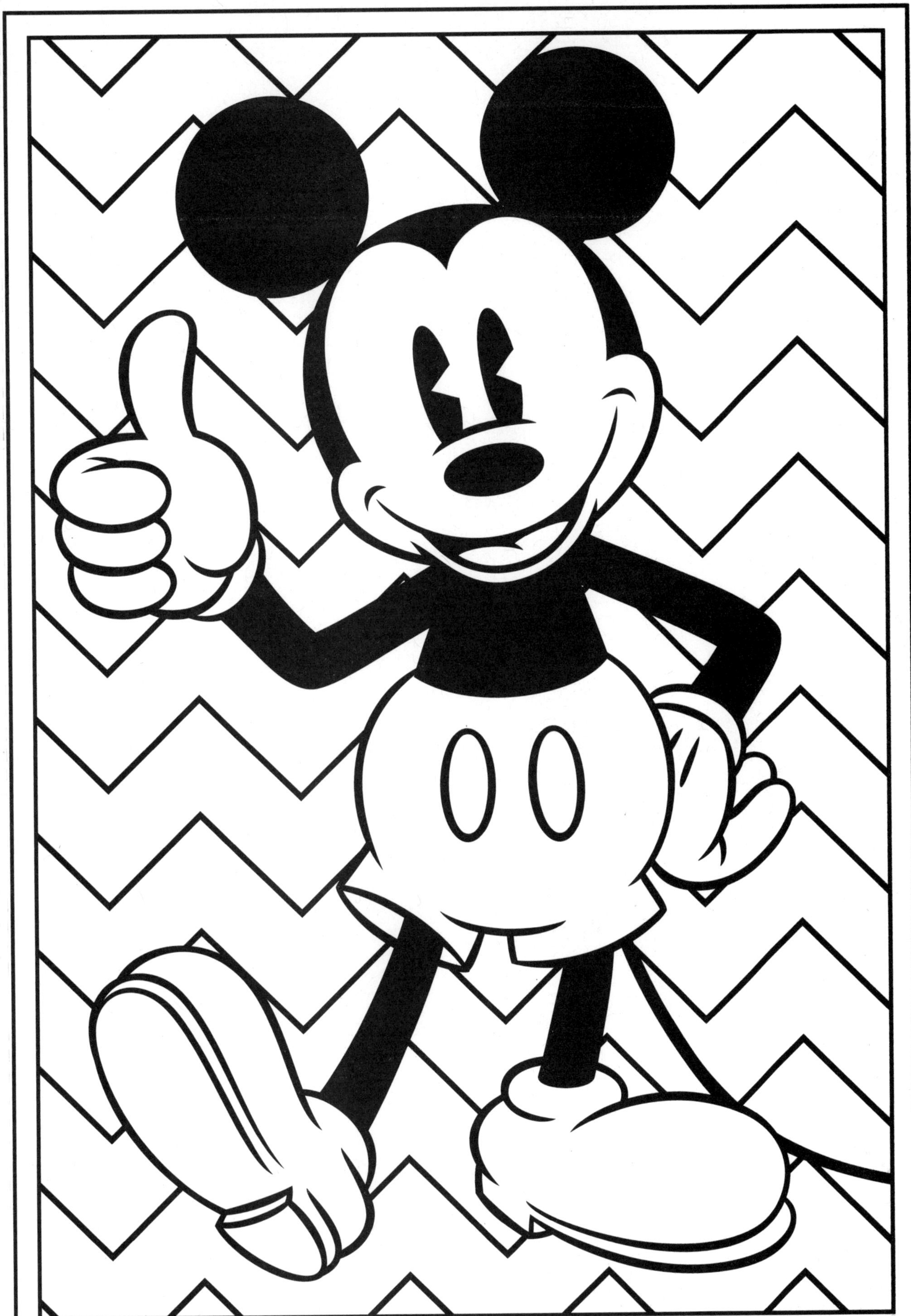

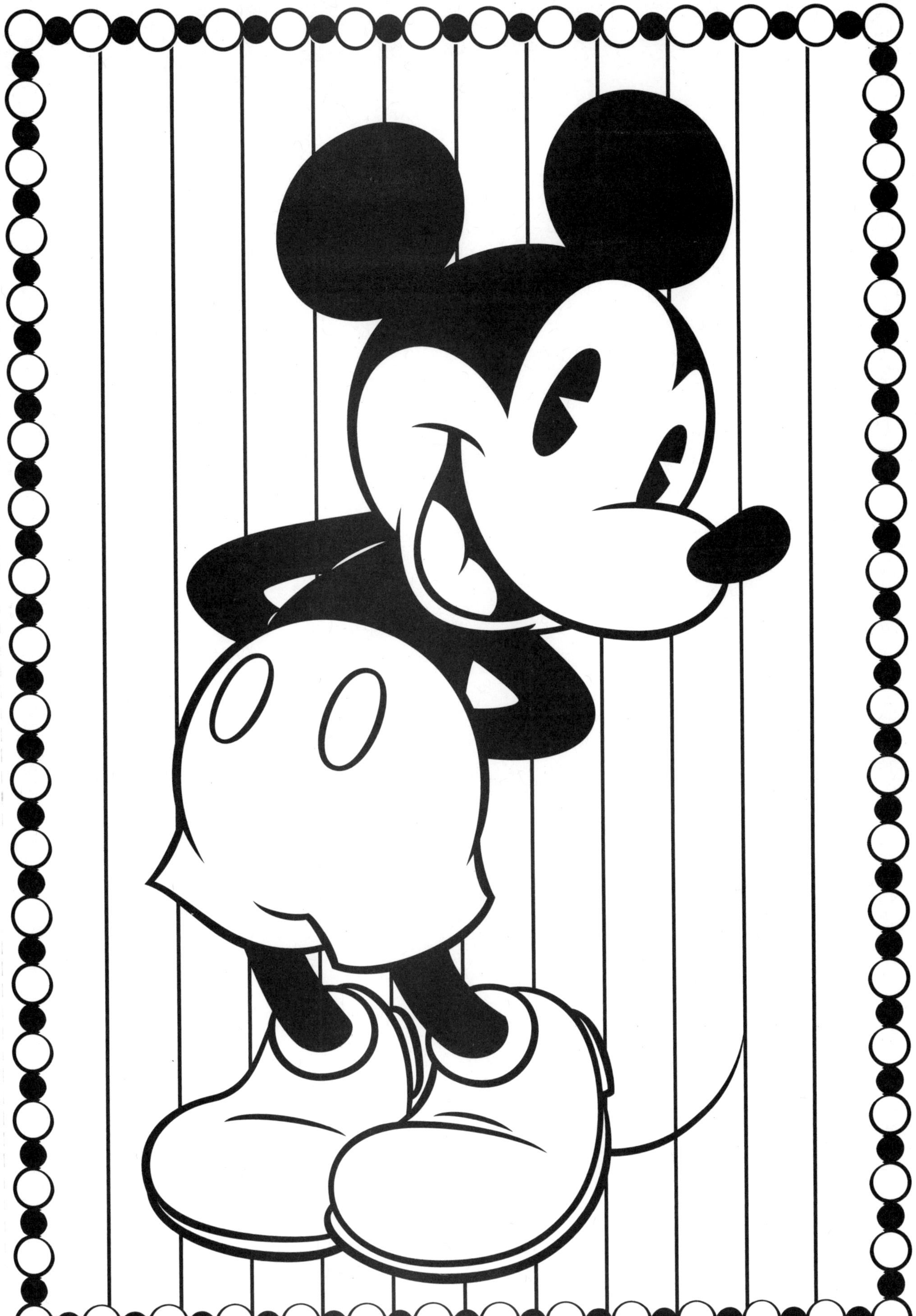

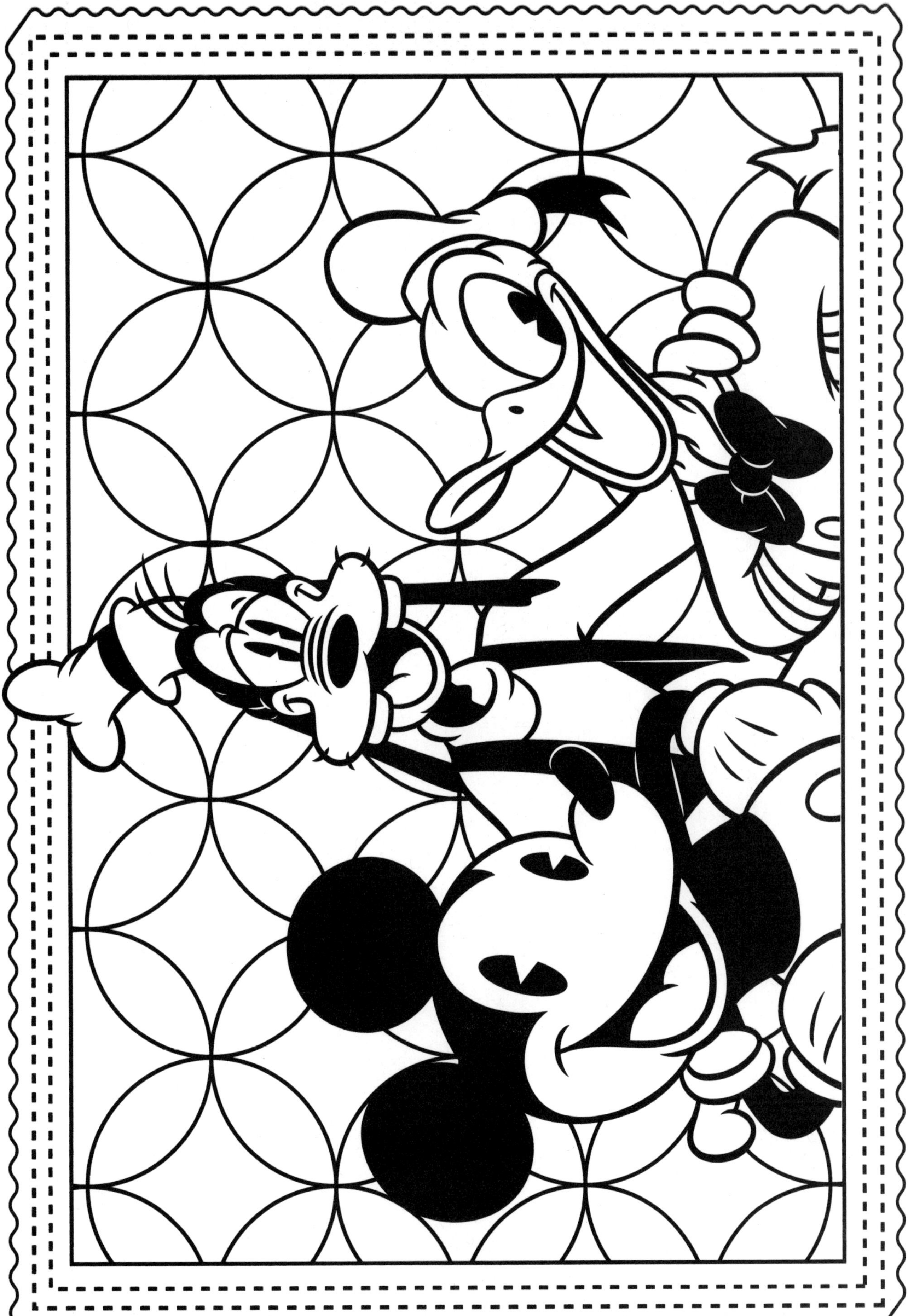

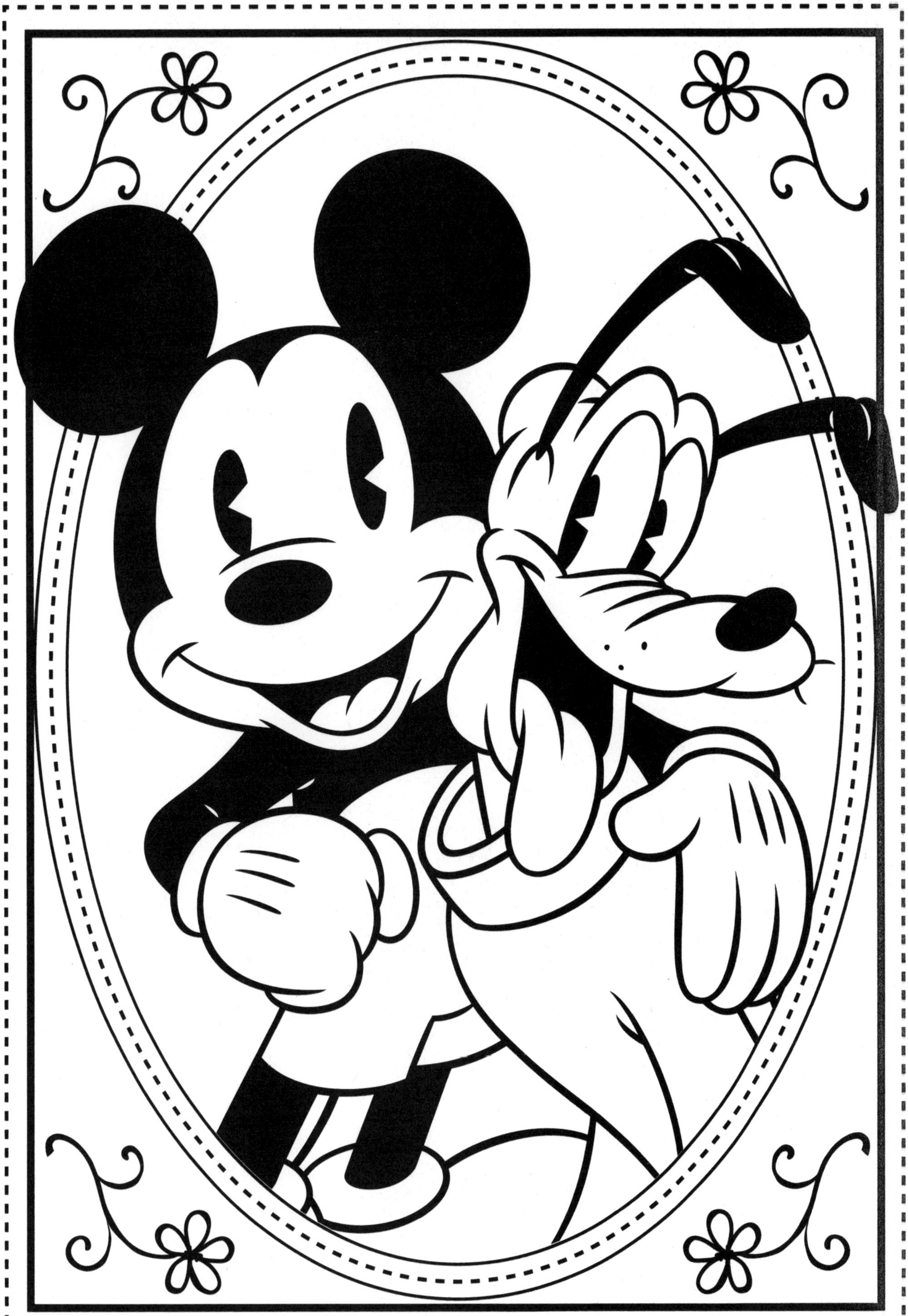

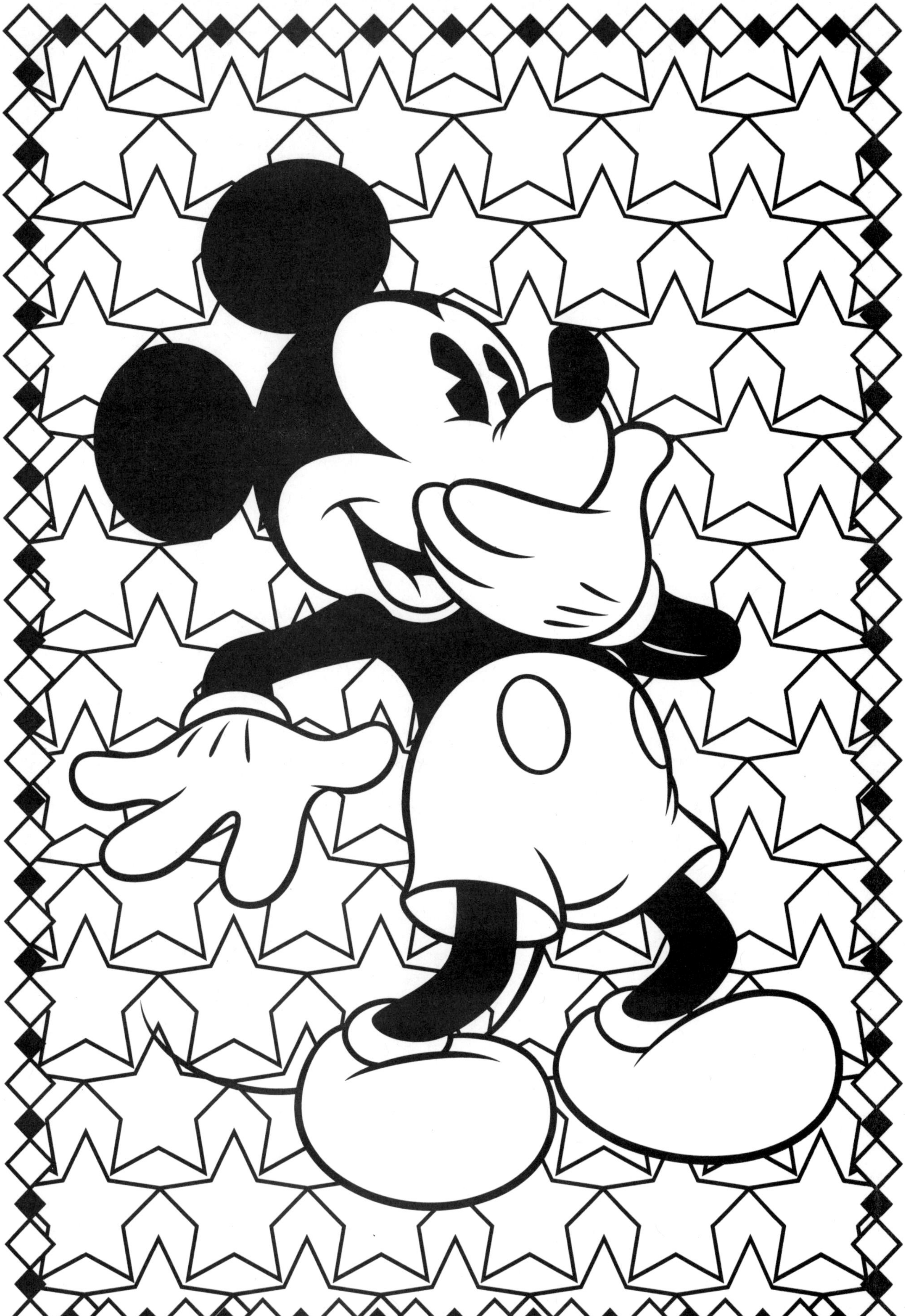

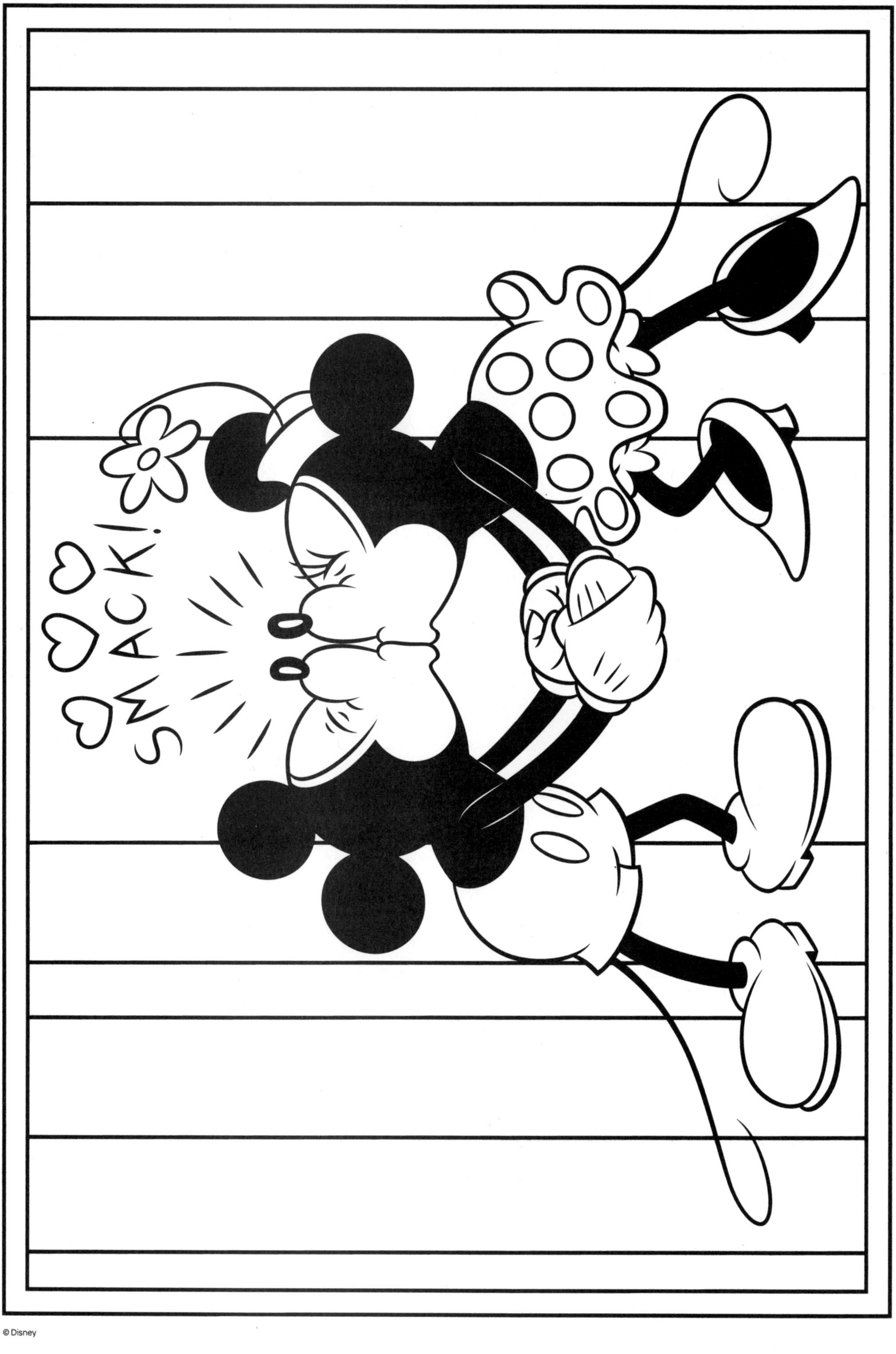
SMACK!

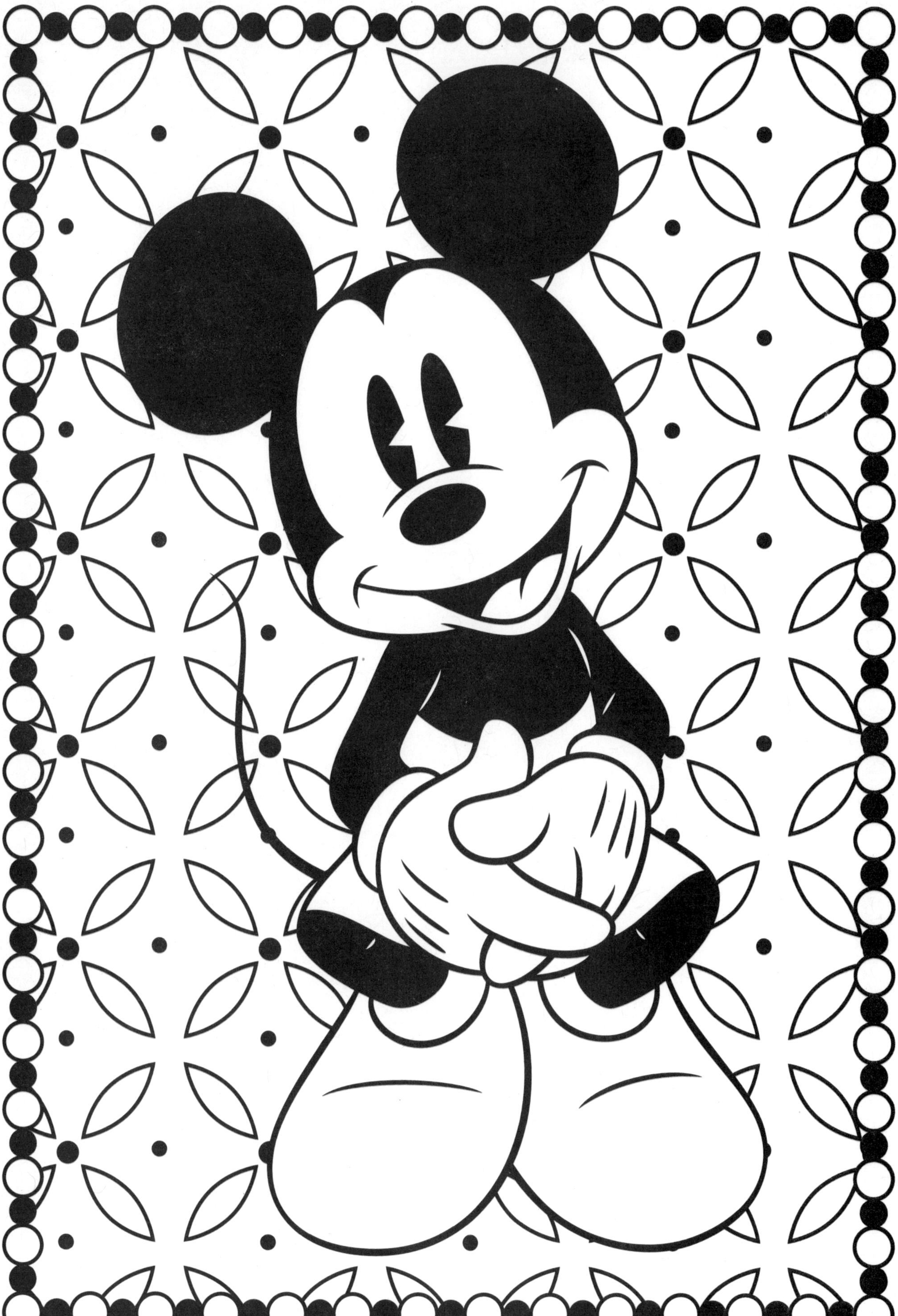

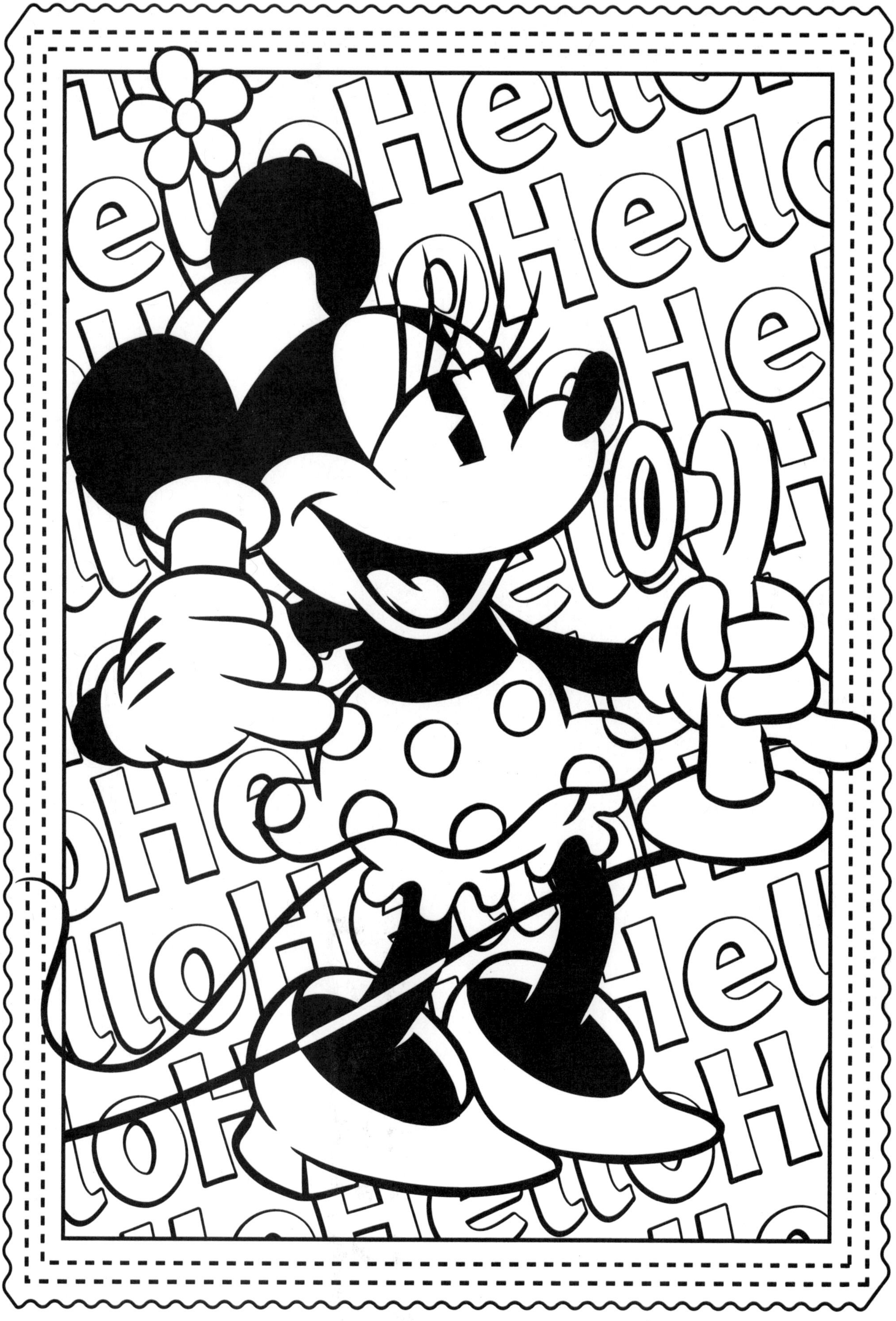

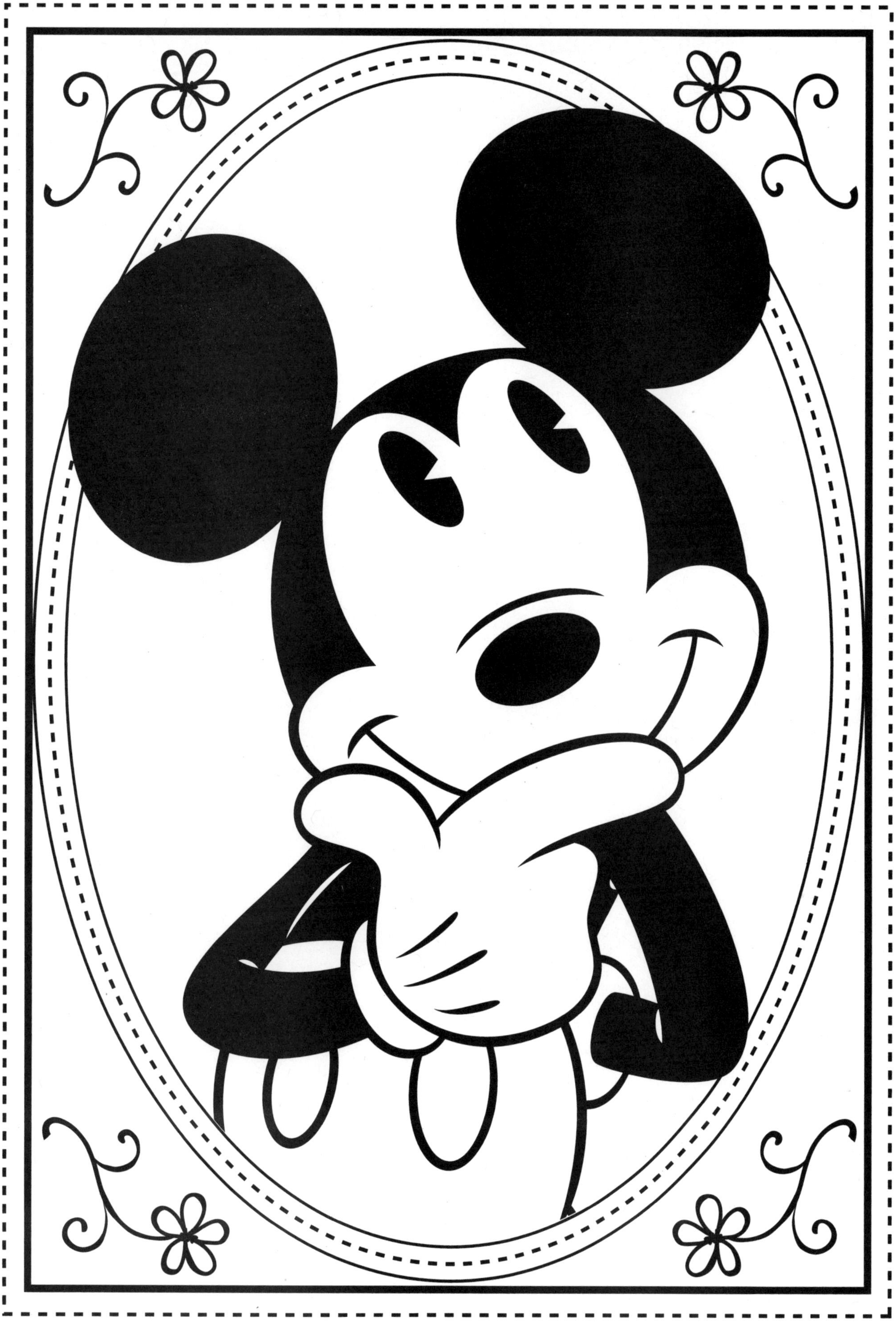

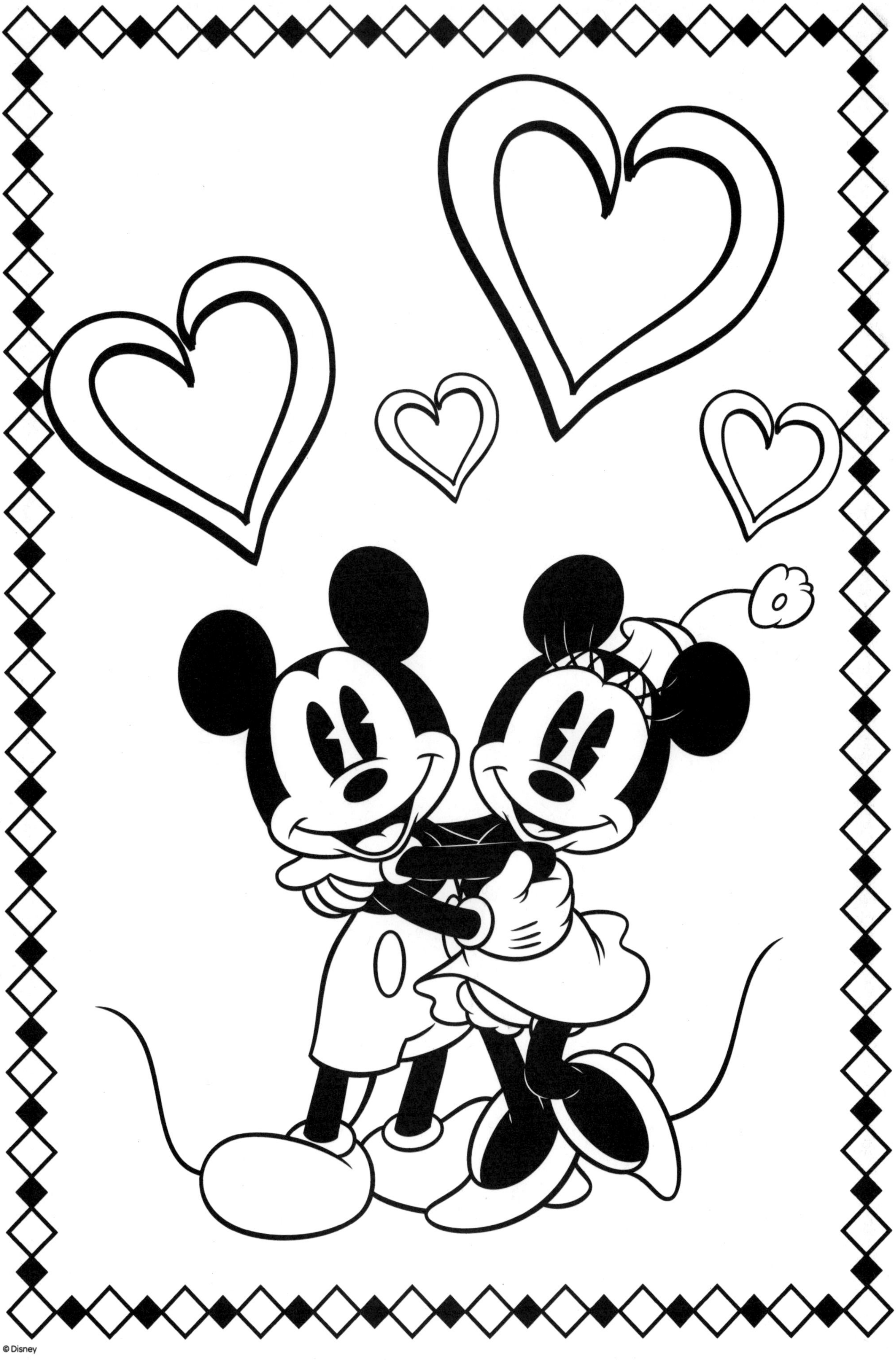

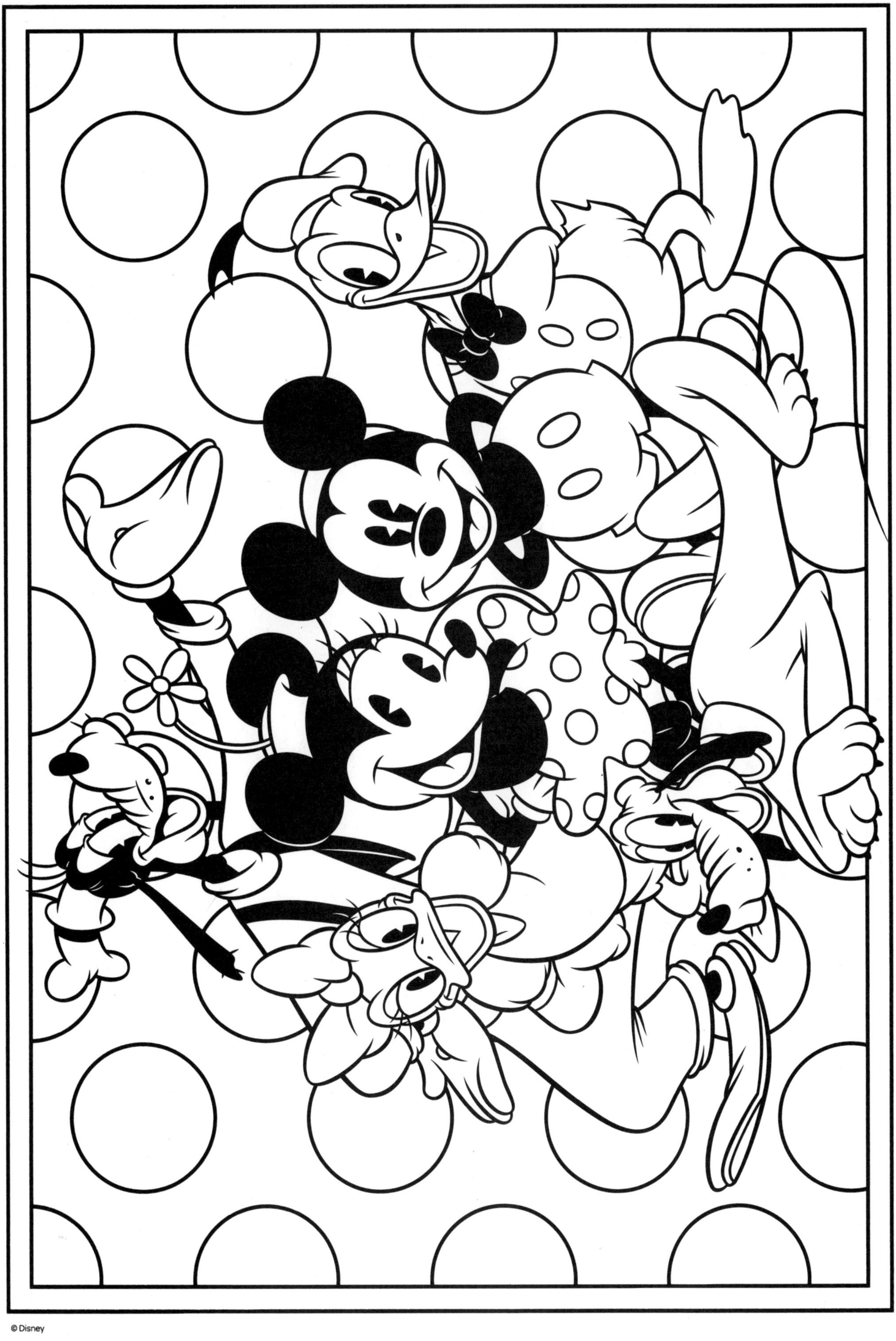

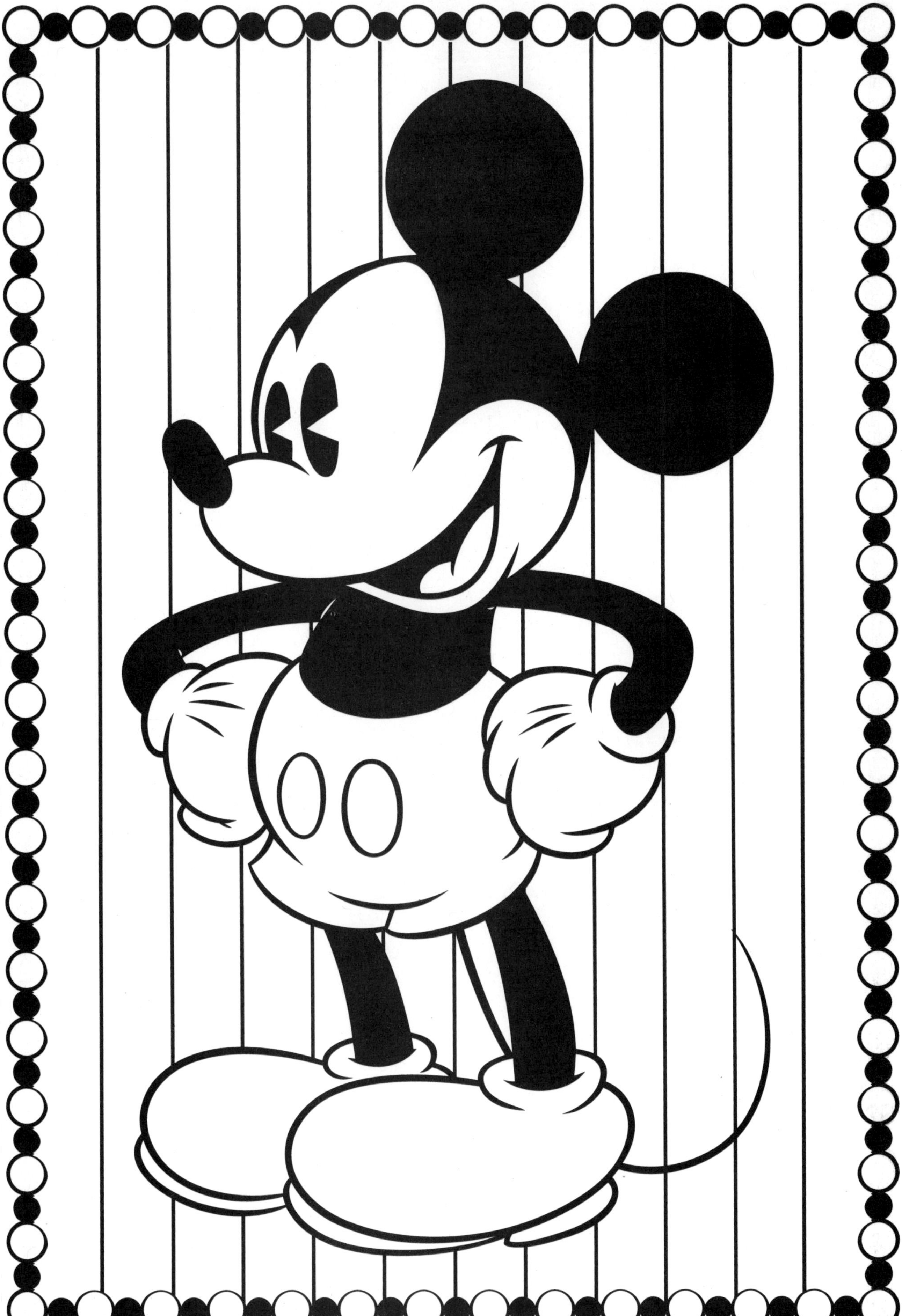

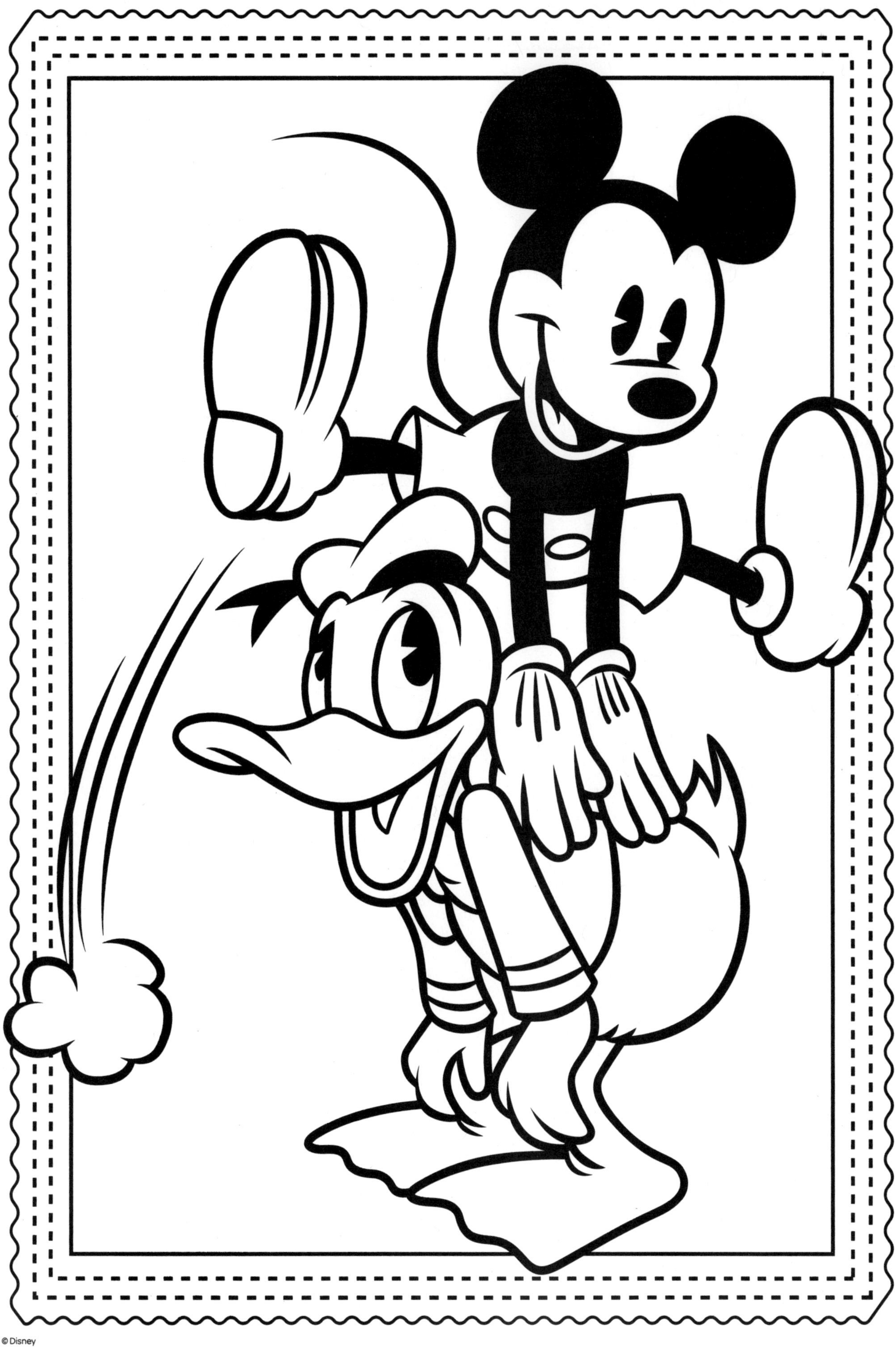

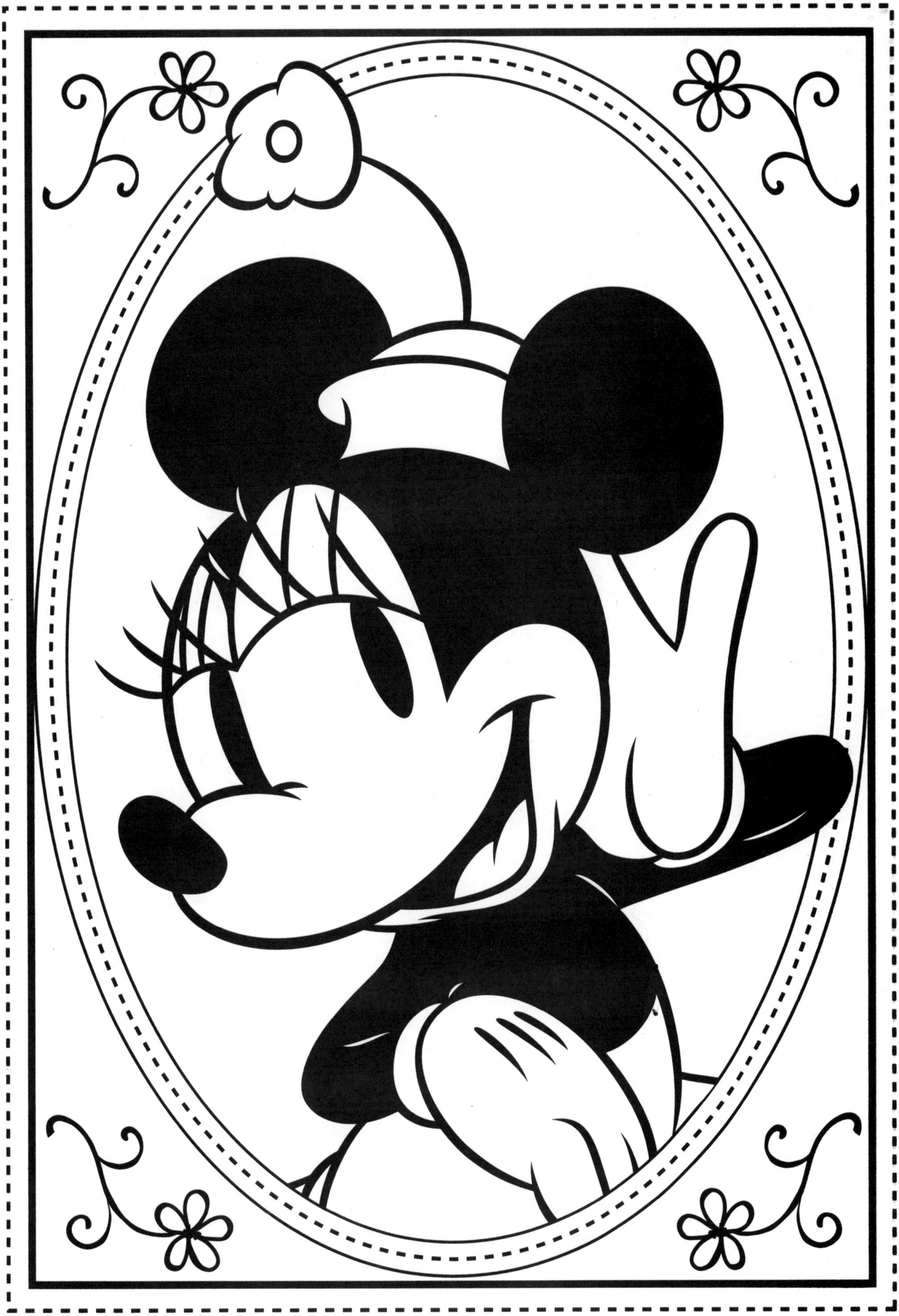

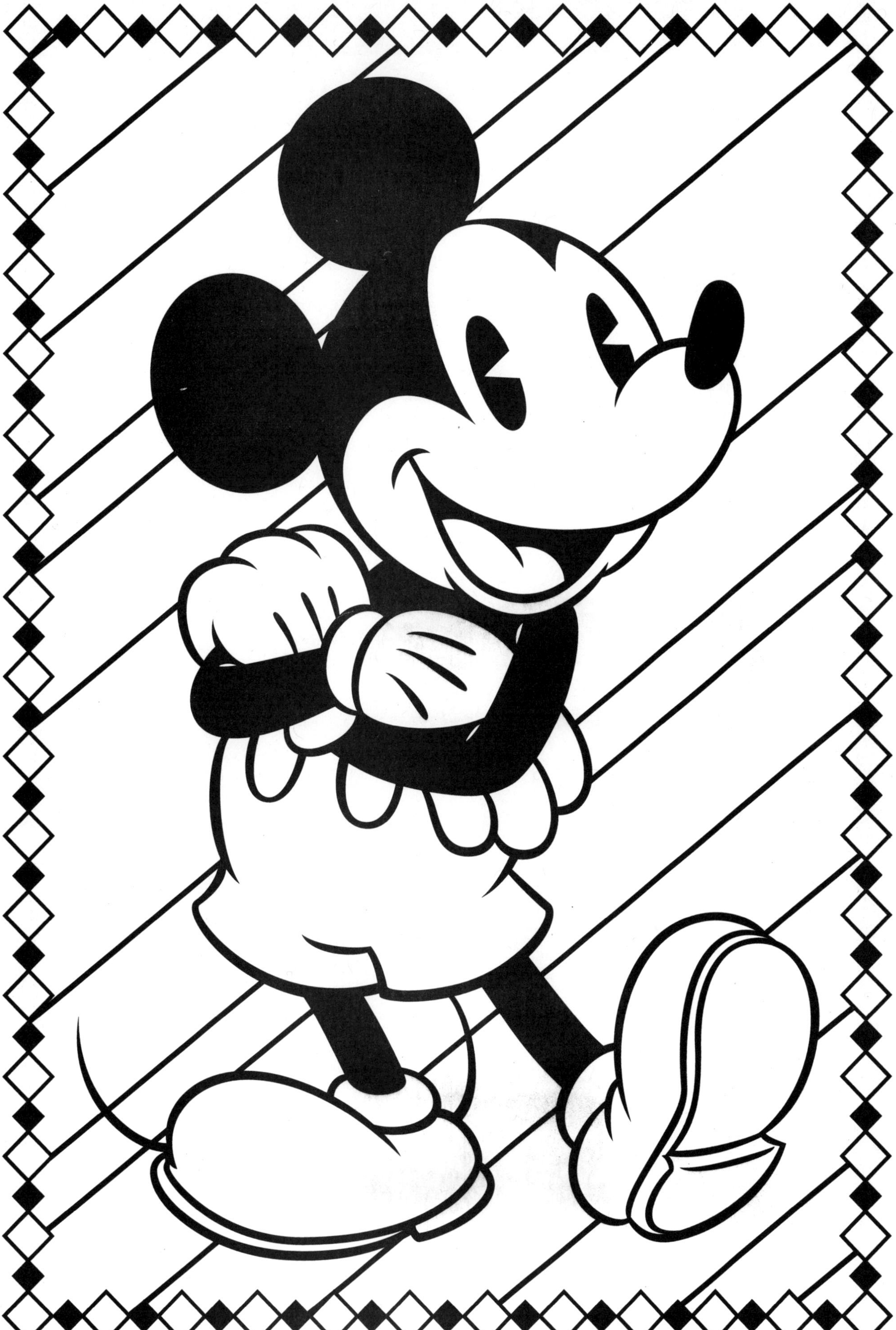